JOHN CLARE
THE LIVING YEAR
1841

JOHN CLARE
THE LIVING YEAR
1841

Edited by Tim Chilcott

TRENT EDITIONS

Published by Trent Editions, 1999

Trent Editions
Department of English and Media Studies
The Nottingham Trent University
Clifton Lane
Nottingham NG11 8NS

Printed in Great Britain by Goaters Limited, Nottingham
ISBN 0 905 488 55 5

Contents

Introduction

When, on 29 December 1841, John Clare was taken from his home at Northborough to begin his second and long, final asylum in Northampton, one of the most exceptional years in his life came to a close. At the beginning of that year, he was a patient in Matthew Allen's comparatively humane and enlightened asylum at High Beach in Essex, where he had lived for a little over three and a half years. Seven months later, in July 1841, he escaped from High Beach and walked the ninety or so miles out of Essex back to Northborough. Certain that he would there be reunited with his childhood sweetheart, Mary Joyce, he did not believe his wife Patty when she told him that Mary was already dead. By December of the year, his mental condition had worsened sufficiently for two doctors to be able to endorse a committal to Northampton General Lunatic Asylum. Against the backcloth of these overt events, he continued to write as prolifically as ever: nearly 1,600 lines of original poetry and a further 1,500 of biblical paraphrase, in addition to letters, natural history observations, and an autobiographical account of his journey from High Beach to Northborough. And at different times as the year advanced, tortured clutches at a sense of dissolving identity were counterpointed against perceptions of complete clarity and ordinariness. For Clare, 1841 was a year lived with what may now seem a special urgency, a particular fullness of need and response.

This is a book that tries to capture, for the first time, the many shapes and contours of this single year in Clare's imaginative life. Although all the material presented here has been previously published in one edition or another, it has never before been seen in this distinctive and important way: as a chronological sequence of drafts and copies that follows as closely as possible the evolution of his poetry and prose, as the spring of 1841 heightened into summer, summer drifted into autumn, and autumn to winter. Beginning with the early stanzas of his Byronic 'imitation', *Child Harold*, and the first of his biblical paraphrases, the evolution moves through the drafting of *Don Juan*, the continuation of *Child Harold*, the prose accounts of the escape from High Beach and of later autumnal scenes, and finally the return to biblical paraphrase and the later stanzas of *Child*

Harold. As this progress is traced, what begins to emerge with growing force are the conjunctions and disjunctions of his imagination, as an image or mood or perception is juxtaposed against another, which in turn is placed (or displaced) within the context of another. At one moment, there may be close parallels of language or form or tone; at the next, strong, even violent, oppositions. This book is therefore a record of changes rather than conclusions, of the processes of writing rather than the final products. At its centre lies the weaving movement of Clare's mind as he responded to a momentous year.

Given the biographical circumstances of imprisonment, escape, return to a home that appeared 'homeless', re-incarceration, it is scarcely surprising that the text of Clare's imaginative response during these twelve months has come to seem more than usually problematic. Indeed, in several ways, the holograph manuscripts of the year define with special concentration the questions and problems posed to all students of his work. As with many of his manuscripts throughout his career, his handwriting is often intricate, sometimes ambiguous, not infrequently faded or otherwise obscured. His spelling is less than perfect, and his punctuation minimal or non-existent. Moreover, the early versions and reworked copies of this year are scattered, often haphazardly, among no fewer than nine separate manuscripts: notebooks, foolscap volumes, covers of exercise books, margins of newspapers. Advertisements, mathematical calculations, memoranda of books lent, unfinished letters, are interleaved between drafts of poetry and prose. Different poems interrupt each other, or are interrupted by quotations from other writers and sources. Almost any page can present substantial difficulties of decipherment, transcription, precedence, and organisation.

It is worth examining these features in a little detail, because they can radically affect the interpretations made of Clare's work during this year. Since the 1960s, few editions have failed to address the question of how best to transcribe his manuscripts, though with very different results. A number have attempted as close and accurate a rendering of his words as possible, retaining for example both ampersands and mis-spellings. Some have corrected spellings and added 'light' punctuation where meaning would be otherwise obscured. Others have retained mis-spellings where they are aurally justified, and derived from the distinctive accents of Northamptonshire dialect. Others, still, have amended all solecisms and presented the work as a 'reading text' following accepted grammar, spelling and punctuation. As I have argued elsewhere,[1] the case for a 'pure' or 'primitive' text of Clare has never seemed to me proven, particularly when raw and sometimes inchoate drafts were painstakingly prepared for publication, and discussed in letter after letter between him and his publisher, John Taylor. The notion that 'first is best', and that 'raw Clare' is always 'authentic Clare' (though authentic to what?), has often led to over-simplifications of the complex historical, imaginative and social processes by which all literature is promulgated. But Clare's work of 1841 occupies a special position in his development. There was no shaping mediation between him and a publisher or editor. Indeed, his texts were not subject, even, to the influence of a contemporary copyist, as with the later, sometimes over-punctuated asylum transcriptions of W.F. Knight. Of all the periods in his long writing career, 1841 seems one of the years in which he talked, as it were, most with himself. It has therefore seemed appropriate to present his actual words as closely as possible to the holograph manuscripts. It has long been argued that the distinctive syntactic freedoms in his work, to take one example, become imaginatively more authoritative when unencumbered by the ordering of 'normal' punctuation. But more significantly for this book, the solecisms enhance that sense of a living process of the imagination – the flows and checks of sometimes untidy creation – rather than the final polish of a definitive version, ready for publication. Clare's words are, then, presented here as accurately as possible, without any emendation of his grammar, spelling, punctuation or capitalisation. The only changes made, if such they can be called, have been to expand certain typographical spacings: between sentences in the prose, and between those contractions of pronoun and verb that might be confused with other words (I'll, he'll, she'd, ye'll, for example, which Clare invariably writes as Ill, hell, shed, yell, consequently read I ll, he ll, she d, ye ll).

If editorial policy about transcription has been a major debating issue, no less has the question of 'authority' between earlier and later versions of the same material. In the autumn of 1841, Clare began to copy a substantial amount of already drafted poetry into a new foolscap volume that he had started immediately upon his return home. A good deal of this copying resulted in only minor changes to the original versions: the occasional word altered, the odd phrase added or omitted. Even in longer pieces, such as the satire *Don Juan* or the paraphrases of *Job*, drafts and copies remained substantively the same. But in the longest work, *Child Harold*, the changes were much more considerable. Here, Clare began to rearrange the sequencing of stanzas, producing a new order in individual verses. 'Began to rearrange', however, is a phrase advisedly used, for the process produced its own confusions. In numbering one extended sequence of stanzas, for example, he began with the number 3 (omitting 1 and 2 altogether), wrote the figure 18 above two separate verses, placed 27 at a markedly earlier point than 26, and did not number three stanzas at all. This entire sequence, moreover, comprising about a third of the total poem, was never copied out from its original form, very probably being interrupted by his enforced removal to Northampton in late December.

The editorial perplexity that has resulted from this unfinished process can be exemplified in two illustrations, which could be multiplied without difficulty. In four different versions of *Child Harold*,[2] *not one* of a hundred stanzas is placed in exactly the same numerical position in the sequence. A verse taken at random ('The Paigles Bloom In Shower's In Grassy Close'), for example, is stanza no. 1 in one version, no. 36 in another, no. 70 in a further, and no. 46 in the last. Equally manifest differences are apparent in interpretations of Clare's textual 'intentions'. For some, an explicit spring-summer-autumn-winter symbolic form can be discerned, based on the assumption that he appeared 'to have planned it as a poem of four cantos'.[3] For others, the assumption of a conscious seasonal frame-work is supererogatory,[4] the seasonal references being no more than Clare's immediate response to the time of writing. For some, the unfinished 'copy' has the status of a 'fair copy', with the result that stanzas written *after* his return home precede those written *before* his escape.[5] For others, such an arrangement seriously erodes a temporal framework, producing a poem that begins in summer and ends in spring.[6]

Given these uncertainties, there are distinct advantages in presenting the various parts of *Child Harold* as closely as possible to the time of their composition. Not only does such an arrangement highlight qualities of process and evolution, but it also establishes an imaginative coherence that draws upon primary patterns of seasonal growth, fruition, and decay. Whether that coherence was consciously planned by Clare, or not, becomes almost immaterial beside the fact that it demonstrably exists. Whether as deliberate symbolic under-pinning or as simple response to the changing seasons, or indeed as both, the spring-summer-autumn-winter progression provides a natural and unforced structure to the poem.

The evidence for dating the material drafted during the year can be divided into five major areas:

i) *characteristic imaginative mode*
   the unalloyed immediacy and directness of Clare's creative response, features that underpin much of his writing,[7] often indicate a specific period of composition. A considerable number of lines are firmly located within present time, with references to individual seasons or months:

'the retireing solitudes of May', 'the glooms of the midsummer even', 'the autumn morn', and so on. The sense of present-time perception is heightened by repetitions of the adverb 'now', in ways stronger than those of mere formulaic apostrophe: 'Now Come The Balm & Breezes Of The Spring', 'Now melancholly autumn comes anew', 'Now harvest browns the fen', ''Tis autumn now', and so forth. Such references are further supported by the mention of specific plants, flowers, soil and weather conditions: 'The Paigles Bloom', 'the white thorn bushes', 'the sloe & dewberry', 'brimming dykes & naked fields'. Elsewhere, direct allusions to contemporary social and political events (such as Whig defeats, elections, and local weddings in *Don Juan*) establish reliable datings during the year.

ii) autobiographical reference
    closely allied to external allusions are internal references with a clear autobiographical focus. Such references can point not only to a general pre- or post-escape period ('& still Im in prison', 'still the forest is round me') but also to more specific moments ('Night finds me on this lengthening road alone', 'I've wandered many a weary mile').

iii) specific dating
    a number of dates are explicitly provided by Clare himself, or can be reliably inferred from his phrasing. The earliest recorded date in the year's material is 17 March (a letter to Patty Clare) and the latest 12 December (a brief journal record 'Found a Cowslip in flower'). Over thirty such explicit dates appear in the poems and prose of the year.

iv) typographical individuality
    Clare's habit of capitalising the first letter of *all* words informs every piece of extant dated material between 17 March and 1 May. It seems very likely that such 'upper-casing' characterised all his writing between early March and mid-May, and that the capitalised stanzas of *Child Harold* can therefore be reliably ascribed to this period.[8]

v) position in manuscript
    although the physical position of any specific material in the manuscripts often helps little in dating, since Clare rarely worked methodically through the pages of his notebooks, certain 'runs' of stanzas in *Child Harold* and *Don Juan* can be established, corresponding to a chronological sequence.

Both singly, and in combination with each other, these features provide the evidence for the known, probable, and possible datings offered in this book. In the text, *known* dates are simply indicated in bold: **15 July**. *Probable* dates are indicated in bold within square brackets: **[May – June]**. *Possible* dates are indicated in bold within square brackets, followed by a question mark: **[September?]**. The notes at the end of the book expand upon particular aspects of dating.

Based on this evidence, the sequence of the nine manuscripts that Clare wrote during the year, with the earliest and latest dates of use, is:

Northampton MS 8 **February – early autumn**
The inscription on p.1, 'John Clares Poems/Feby 1841', indicates the earliest time at which he was using this volume. A stanza from *Child Harold* ('Now melancholly autumn comes anew') suggests the manuscript was still in use until September or October of the year.

Northampton MS 7 **18 June – early autumn**
Drafts in the margins of *The Morning Chronicle* dated 18 June point to the earliest date of use during 1841. It seems probable, however, that most, if not all, of the material in this manuscript was composed after his return home on 24 July. Both explicit and implicit references suggest a post-escape period. A *Child Harold* stanza ('Now harvest smiles') and the lines 'O when will autumn bring the news/Now harvest browns the fen' indicate the volume was still in use until early autumn.

Peterborough MS D20 **[24 July – early autumn?]**
It seems certain that these drafts on the cover of an exercise book belonging to one of Clare's sons could have been written only after his return home on 24 July. The latest date of use is probably early autumn.

Bodleian MS Don.a.8 **27 August/3 September – late autumn**
Drafts in the margins of *The Lincolnshire Chronicle and General Advertiser* for 27 August, and of *The Lincoln Rutland and Stamford Mercury* for 3 September, identify the earliest date of composition. The latest period of use is probably October or possibly November.

Peterborough MS A62 **[October? – late December]**
Explicit references to mid-autumnal scenes suggest October as the earliest month of use. Some brief natural history notes are dated 19 October, 4 November and 12 December. The latest possible date of use is 29 December, when Clare was taken to Northampton Asylum.

Bodleian MS Don.c.64   **[October? – late December]**
It seems probable that October is the earliest period of use for this
manuscript. Extensive biblical paraphrases are interrupted by a poem
written on 11 November, and there are several explicit references to
winter scenes. The latest date of use is 29 December.

Northampton MS 6   **24 July – late December**
It was into this volume that Clare copied much of the material in the
manuscripts above. The earliest date of use is indicated by two *Child
Harold* songs, written 'directly after' his arrival in Northborough. The
period during which most of the material was transcribed is uncertain,
and some of it may have been contemporaneous with newly drafted
poems and prose in the manuscripts above. On balance, it seems likely
that much of the copying took place later rather than earlier (i.e. later
October, November and December, rather than August, September and
early October). The transcribing was almost certainly interrupted by his
removal to Northampton.

In addition to these seven major sources, *Northampton MS 30* and
Northampton MS 419 contain, respectively, the text of a letter to Patty
Clare dated 17 March, and to George Reid dated 17 November.

These manuscripts, then, provide the complete text of Clare's responses,
both imaginative and domestic, to his experience during 1841. In an ideal
world, the fullest and most accurate way of enacting the detailed, living
processes of composition might well be to present each holograph and a
printed transcription on a weekly and even daily basis, following the draft
of the stanza written that morning with the letter written later in the day,
the calculation of finances made the following afternoon, and so on. But
even if such moments in time could be specified, a presentation of this
kind, it is clear, would become impossibly unwieldy, as well as many
volumes long. So that the nature of Clare's responses can be traced as
fluently as possible, two major approaches have therefore been adopted.
First, each *verso* and *recto* page presents, on the left-hand page, the text of
his longest 1841 poem, *Child Harold*, and on the right-hand,
contemporaneous material from *Don Juan*, the biblical paraphrases, or other
poems written during the year. In this way, a glance across from left- to
right-hand page, or *vice versa*, contextualises the drafts, allowing both the
similarities and the differences in his imaginative concerns to appear.
Alternatively, concentration on *verso* or *recto* pages alone allows the evolution
of a single text to be followed. Occasional blank pages indicate a temporary

'lull' in drafting certain stanzas or poems, while the material on the opposite page takes precedence. Secondly, the prose pieces composed during the year (including letters) are separated from the poetry, and appear after it. To have interpolated prose texts into what was already a complex poetic evolution could well have muddied rather than clarified the processes of his imagination. For both poetry and prose, however, the same typographical devices are deployed. The headers on each page identify not only the titles of texts but also the periods of composition in question.

It is now possible to turn to the larger questions of interpretation raised by Clare's work of 1841. What is at once apparent is both its extent and its range. Although his productivity was never less than considerable throughout his career, there seems little doubt that 1841 marks a high point in terms of the sheer amount of material produced. At its baldest, the 3,000 or so lines of poetry from this year represent an average of over eight lines a day, not including the prose writings also. No clear reason emerges why this particular year should have produced such a prolific output,[9] though a good deal of it may be derived from what was, for him, a deep and almost instinctive response. As I have suggested elsewhere,[10] the embedding of his lyrical impulse in a tradition of oral recitation produces a poetry in which repetition is a fundamental and natural imaginative procedure. The realms of love and nature, sorrow and death, are insistent and continually accessible, to be articulated time and again as part of a fully familiar, communal understanding. But Clare's repetitions during this year are not mere prolixity or redundancy. They are counterpointed by a manifest range of experiment, in which markedly different poems are produced. In tone and attitude, for instance, much of *Child Harold* is deeply meditative, weaving a speculative, often indeterminate path between loss and transcendence, the anguish of the separated self and the potential redemption of love. Its primary mode of perception is of unsettled and unsettling half-lights, a world haunted by the private shadows of paradox and ambiguity, both involuntary and deliberate. *Don Juan*, on the other hand, is violently and pruriently satiric, exposing a world of sexual licence, social sham, and political and religious cant, where all value has been irretrievably undermined. The intimacies of *Child Harold* are drowned out by a loud, public voice – knowing, self-dramatising, willing to subvert even its own accents. Then again, the biblical paraphrases stand in radical opposition to such subversion, embracing a fierce, largely Old Testament[10] surety in elemental truths: sorrow, faith, covenant, mercy, redemption. The human prayers of David and Solomon, Job and Jeremiah, are voiced into an almost primordial universe of catastrophic force: eternal thunder, apocalyptic lightning, the geological time of rock and water. Yet in contrast to this cosmic stage, the prose evocations of autumnal scenes around Northborough are infinitely more muted and localised, endorsing the simple sanctity of known, commonplace things – this piece of grass, that river, this whitethorn hedge. At one edge of the range, a simple observation at a particular place on a particular day ('Octr 19. 1841 – William found a Cowslip in flower'); at the other, a realm infinitely beyond all human time and place, the chaos before creation. If Clare were not known as the author of all this material, it would at the very least be feasible to argue that several different hands were at work.

It would of course be easy to see in these imaginative collisions a reflection of his own mental crisis during 1841. And certainly, the turbulent shifts in tone and theme are given particular emphasis when, as in this book, they are placed together visually, as palpable contrasts between left and right-hand page. It becomes clear that within days, possibly even within hours, he could move from the sexual bravura of *Don Juan* to the love poetry of *Child Harold*. On 11 July, to take the most clearly dated contrast, he wrote stanzas for *Don Juan* in which Byron's identity, and birthday, were confused with his own; four days later on 15 July, he evoked the transcendently assured identity of 'I live in love sun of undying light' in a poem for *Child Harold*. Despite these and similar contrasts, nevertheless, it would be misleading to present the work of 1841 simply in terms of vast imaginative leaps from cosmos to cowslip. Alongside such dramatic antitheses, patterns persist, a sense of a shaping evolution that informs, and even underpins, the variety of the year's creativity.

Its early stages – from February until about midsummer – are characterised by a sharp, angular, imaginative energy that seems to thrust towards the edges of things, experimenting with their potential, testing their boundaries and limits. As already mentioned, typographical conventions are eroded with a code that consistently capitalises the first letter of every word, whether in poem or letter, advertisement or descriptive prose. The capitalisation continues until about mid-May when, in the middle of two separate poems, which are placed side by side in this text, it is suddenly jettisoned in favour of normal upper and lower cases, never to reappear. Key words in his vocabulary ('be', 'love', 'live', 'hope', 'sun', 'heart') drive the verse forward, often in fractured patterns of antithesis and overthrow: blooms/fades, prison/free, live/die, hopeless/hope, Satan/Paradise. Identities collide, dissolve and re-emerge in vital challenges to the world: from the poet Byron–Clare, through the husband with two wives, to the prize fighter Jack Randall. The battles of faith in the early Old Testament paraphrases give way to the sexual licence and political diatribes of *Don Juan*. And throughout, there is the yearning drive to move beyond the 'chain of contradictions' towards unifying context and validation, whether of home, or family, or Mary Joyce, or poetry. The work of these months is tense with argument, debate, even obsession.

But after the escape from High Beach in July, and the slow, wrenching realisation that Mary will never be found again, a more reflective, ruminative voice is heard, as the imaginative energies of spring and early summer become muted. Time begins to haunt the poetry, especially in the continuation of *Child Harold*. Images from the past (hedge, church spire, meadow, schoolyard) crowd into memory, as the 'map of boyhood' is traced but becomes 'overcast'. The act of remembering takes on an increasingly ambiguous role, on the one hand affirming the value of the past, on the other serving only to accentuate the separation between what has gone and what remains. Not that time present is entirely devoid of significance. Many of the scenes of autumn continue to be evoked with the same scrupulous accuracy, the same sense of knowledge and confirmation, as in much of his earlier work. But at the same time, natural images are perceived as diffuse, fluctuating, elusive – products of 'seeming' rather than 'seeing'. The figure of Mary defines the uncertainty. She is both 'faithless' and 'divine', both 'hell' and 'heaven', the pole star of his 'being' and 'decay'. She is always present, but never there – not in Northborough, in his cottage, with him.

As the autumn of 1841 slows into winter, a numbing internalisation of response seems to become ever more prevalent. Occasional material, it is true, continues to hearken back to ancient affirmations and verities – paraphrases of the Psalms, St Matthew's vision of the Last Judgment, the Book of Revelations – but the emphasis falls increasingly upon a dulled, frozen self, insensible to the world of vital objects. The opening and closing lines of what is almost certainly his last biblical paraphrase (of *Isaiah* ch. 47) evoke the isolation: 'Come down & sit in dust' and 'There's none shall be able to shield thee or save thee'. The desolation is echoed in the few, spare last stanzas of *Child Harold*. A *Winterreise*-like image of the wanderer, bereft of both friend and home, haunts the verse. Nature, love, family have all been neutralised into a grey, spectral non-identity. A quatrain in the final song summarises the momentous change:

> Her truth & heart was once my home
> & May was all the year
> But now through seasons as I roam
> Tis winter everywhere

Four days after Christmas, the 'winter everywhere' became complete.

What is presented in this book is, then, a process not only of seasonal, but also of mental and emotional, change. It would of course be tempting to argue that these outer and inner worlds were closely, even causally, related – that the natural growth of the spring and summer of 1841 became reflected in the energies and experiments of the High Beach poetry, just as the decay of autumn and winter was echoed in the later Northborough work. But such an equation is fraught with imponderables, not least the complex and problematic relationship between the 'mind of Clare' and 'the mind in Clare's poetry'. The two states are not synonymous. It is worth remembering, too, that the winter of 1841 was far from the end of his poetic career. Indeed, in several respects, the constantly modulating perceptions of *Child Harold* or *Don Juan* – that sense of awareness being as much fashioned by the perceiver as by the things perceived – can be seen as a prelude to the more sustainedly internalised poetry he was to write in Northampton Asylum. But the winter brought an especially distilled and fertile experience to a close. In personal terms, 1841 was for Clare a year of particular urgency and wretchedness. But it was too a year that was recorded, and dated, and memorialised. And in that creative shaping of a human hurt, it was also an *annus mirabilis*.

Tim Chilcott
Brighton, Sussex
July 1999

Acknowledgements

Like any student of Clare, I am greatly indebted to all those editors, interpreters and keepers of his work who have secured such firm foundations to support new inquiry. It would be invidious to select from the list of names in the notes and in the further reading section; but each editor and critic mentioned there has helped in some way to clarify, sharpen, and deepen my own thinking about Clare. I acknowledge, equally, the care of the librarians in Northampton Public Library, Peterborough Museum, the Bodleian Library and the University of Sussex library. Two names, however, deserve to be mentioned for their personal engagement in the spirit of free exchange that should characterise all discussions of Clare. Cathy Taylor, whose doctoral research into the 1841 manuscripts valuably complements this book, has shared her text and transcriptions; and it is particularly pleasing to record discussions that have been so full, generous and co-operative. Similarly, John Goodridge at Nottingham Trent University has given constant help and advice, and for his unfailing support and encouragement over many months I am very grateful indeed. If, though, there should be a dedication to this book, it should go ungrudgingly, not to past or present students of Clare, but to those of the future. Some, perhaps many, of them are yet unknown. But it is they who will carry his name forward.

THE POETRY OF 1841

2

CHILD HAROLD
[early spring – mid? May]

[early spring – mid? May]

4¹

Now Come The Balm & Breezes Of The Spring
Not With The Pleasure's Of My Early Day's
When Nature Seemed One Endless Song To Sing
A Joyous Melody & Happy Praise
Ah Would They Come Agen – But Life Betrays
Quicksands & Gulphs & Storms That Howl & Sting
All Quiet Into Madness & Delays
Care Hides the Sunshine With Its Raven Wing
& Hell Glooms Sadness Oer The Songs of Spring

5

Like Satans Warcry First in Paradise   10
When Love Lay Sleeping On The Flowery Slope
Like Virtue Wakeing In The Arms Of Vice
Or Deaths Sea Bursting In The Midst Of Hope
Sorrows Will Stay – & Pleasures Will Elope
In The Uncertain Cartnty Of Care
Joys Bounds Are Narrow But A Wider Scope
Is Left For Trouble Which Our Life Must Bear
Of Which All Human Life Is More Or Less The Heir

6

My Mind Is Dark & Fathomless & Wears
The Hues Of Hopeless Agony & Hell   20
No Plummet Ever Sounds The Souls Affairs
There Death Eternal Never Sounds The Knell

30 April

Israel Passing Over The Red Sea [fragment][3]

The Lord He Has Triumphed His People Are Free
The Horse & The Tyrant Are Whelmed In The Sea

8

CHILD HAROLD
[early spring – mid? May]

With Him & Will Be All His Whole Life Long
Lone Child Of Sorrow & Perpetual Wrong   70

10

But Providence That Grand Eternal Calm
Is With Him Like The Sunshine In The Sky
Nature Our Kindest Mother Void Of Harm
Watches The Orphan's Lonely Infancy
Strengthening The Man When Childhoods Care Are Bye
She Nurses Still Young Unreproached Distress
& Hears The Lonely Infants Every Sigh
Who Finds At Length To Make Its Sorrows Less
Mid Earths Cold Curses There Is One To Bless

11

Sweet Rural Maids Made Beautifull By Health   80
Brought Up Where Natures Calm Encircles All
Where Simple Love Remains As Sterling Wealth
Where Simple Habits Early Joys Recall
Of Youthfull Feelings Which No Wiles Enthrall
The Happy Milk Maid In Her Mean Array
Fresh As The New Blown Rose Outblooms Them All
E'en Queens Might Sigh To Be As Blest As They
While Milkmaids Laugh & Sing Their Cares Away

12

How Doth Those Scenes Which Rural Mirth Endears
Revise Old Feelings That My Youth Hath Known   90
& Paint The Faded Bloom Of Earlier Years

BIBLICAL PARAPHRASES
30 April

BIBLICAL PARAPHRASES
30 April

9

CHILD HAROLD
[early spring – mid? May]

& Soften Feelings Petrefied To Stone
Joy Fled & Care Proclaimed Itself My Own
Farewells I Took Of Joys In Earliest Years
& Found The Greatest Bliss To Be Alone
My Manhood Was Eclipsed But Not In Fears
– Hell Came In Curses & She Laugh'd At Tears

13

But Memory Left Sweet Traces Of Her Smiles
Which I Remember Still & Still Endure
The Shadows Of First [Love?]s My Heart Beguiles   100
Time Brought Both Pain & Pleasure But No Cure
Sweet Bessey Maid Of Health & Fancys Pure
How Did I Woo Thee Once – Still Unforgot
But Promises In Love Are Never Sure
& Where We Met How Dear Is Every Spot
& Though We Parted Still I Murmur Not

14

For Loves However Dear Must Meet With Clouds
& Ties Made Tight Get Loose & May Be Parted
Springs First Young Flowers The Winter Often Shrouds
& Loves First Hopes Are Very Often Thwarted   110
E'en Mine Beat High & Then Fell Broken Hearted
& Sorrow Mourned In Verse To Reconscile
My Feelings To My Fate Though Lone & Parteded[3]
Loves Enemies Are Like The Scorpion Vile
That Oer Its Ruined Hopes Will Hiss & Smile

BIBLICAL PARAPHRASES
30 April

CHILD HAROLD
[April – mid? May]

18[4]

There Is A Tale For Every Day To Hear
For Every Heart To Feel & Tongue To Tell
The Daughters Anzious Dread The Lovers Fear
Pains That In Cots & Palaces May Dwell
Not Short & Passing Like The Friends Farewell
Where Tears May Fall & Leave A Smile Beneath
Eternal Grief Rings In The Passing Bell
Tis Not The Sobs Of Momentary Breath
Ties Part Forever In The Tale Of Death

120

15

Yet Love Lives On In Every Kind Of Weather
In Heat & Cold In Sunshine & In Gloom
Winter May Blight & Stormy Clouds May Gather
Nature Invigorates & Love Will Bloom
It Fears No Sorrow In A Life To Come
But Lives Within Itself From Year To Year
As Doth The Wild Flower In Its Own Perfume
As In The Lapland Snows Springs Blooms Appear
So True Love Blooms & Blossoms Every Where

130

[April – mid? May]

27[5]

The Paigles Bloom In Shower's In Grassy Close
How Sweet To Be Among Their Blossoms Led
& Hear Sweet Nature To Herself Discourse
While Pale The Moon Is Bering Over Head

BIBLICAL PARAPHRASES
[April – mid? May]

[April – mid? May]

Song of Deborah[4]
[Judges 5: 6-31]

In The War Days Of Shamgar Of Anath & Jael
When The High Ways Were Leveled & Hamlets Laid Low

CHILD HAROLD
[April – mid? May]

& Hear The Grazeing Cattle Softly Tread
Cropping The Hedgerows Newly Leafing Thorn
Sounds Soft As Visions Murmured Oer In Bed 140
At Dusky Eve Or Sober Silent Morn
For Such Delights Twere Happy Man Was Born

Ballad

The Blackbird Has Built In The Pasture Agen
& The Thorn Oer The Pond Shows A Delicate Green
Where I Strolled With Patty Adown In The Glen
& Spent Summer Evenings & Sundays Unseen
How Sweet The Hill Brow
& The Low Of The Cow
& The Sunshine That Gilded The Bushes So Green
When Evening Brought Dews Natures Thirst To Allay 150
& Clouds Seemed To Nestle Round Hamlets & Farms
While In The Green Bushes We Spent The Sweet Day
& Patty Sweet Patty Was Still In My Arms

The Love Bloom That Redded Upon Her Sweet Lips
The Love Light That Glistened Within Her Sweet Eye
The Singing Bees There That The Wild Honey Sips
From Wild Blossoms Seemed Not So Happy As I
How Sweet Her Smile Seemed
While The Summer Sun Gleamed
& The Laugh Of The Spring Shadowed Joys From On High 160
While The Birds Sung About Us & Cattle Grazed Round
& Beauty Was Blooming On Hamlets & Farms
How Sweet Steamed The Inscence Of Dew From The Ground
While Patty Sweet Patty Sat Locked In My Arms

BIBLICAL PARAPHRASES
[April – mid? May]

& Every Heart Seemed In Its Courage To Fail
& Sought Out The Bye Ways In Fear Of The Foe

The Inhabitants Ceased In Each Village To Dwell
Desolation Drove Comfort From Mountain & Plain
Till I Even Deborah Rose To Foretell
That God Would Unite With His Chosen Again

They Chose Them New Gods With Presumption Elate
Forty Thousand In Israel Without Shield Or Spear   10
Their False Hearted Foeman Hurled War At The Gates
& The Gods Of Their Choice Were Unable To Hear

With The Rulers Of Israel My Heart Would Agree
Who Offered To Serve In The Troops Of The Lord
& Joined With The People To Fall Or Be Free
They Blessed The True God & Met Truth In His Word

Bless Ye The Lord Who Brought Comfort & Peace
Speak Ye That Ride On White Asses & Say
How The God Of Our Sires Brought His People Release
Yet Sit Down In Judgement To Show The Right Way   20

Now They're Delivered From Archers & War
At The Wells Where The Joyous Draw Water & sing
Where Fear Heard The Hoise Of The Archers Afar
& Death Often Crimsoned The Clear Flowing Spring

There Shall They Sing In The Praise Of The Lord
There Shall They Herd & Draw Water In Peace
Each Village Agen Shall Its Comforts Afford
& War In The Valleys Of Israel Shall Cease

The People Of God Shall Go down To The Gate
Awake Awake Deborah Waken & Sing   30

CHILD HAROLD
[April – mid? May]

Ballad[6]

The Rose Of The World Was Dear Mary To Me
In The Days Of My Boyhood & Youth
I Told Her In Songs Where My Heart Wished To Be
& My Songs Where The Language Of Truth

I Told Her In Looks When I Gazed In Her Eyes
That Mary Was Dearest To Me   170
I Told Her In Words & The Language Of Sighs
Where My Whole Hearts Affections Would Be

I Told her in love that all nature was true
I convinced her that nature was kind
But love in his trials had labour to do
[&?] Mary would be in the mind

Mary met me in spring where the speedwell knots grew
& the kingcups were shining like flame
I chose her all colours red yellow & blue
But my love was one hue & the same   180

Spring summer & winter & all the year through
In the sunshine the shower & the blast
I told the same tale & she knows it all true
& Mary's my blossom at last

BIBLICAL PARAPHRASES
[April – mid? May]

Lead Captivity Captive Thou Barak Too Great
Is Israel For Chuseing The Lord For Their King

Then Him That Remaineth right constant & true
He Made Have Dominion Oer Nobles & peers
The Lord He Made Me Have dominion & Shew
To Govern The Mighty nor hearken to Fears

Out Of Ephraim was there even a root
Went out against Amalek faceing the foe
After Benjamin Thou That wert swifter of foot
& Thy People to join were not tardy Or slow   40

Out of Machir Came Governors ready to Serve
Out of Zebulun they that could handle the Pen
The princes of Issacah They That Deserve
The protection of God & the praises of men

Barak went down To The valley on foot
While Deborah led forward & cheared on the fray
But for Reuben's divisions the soldiers was smote
There was great thought of heart on that terrible day

Why abide in the sheepfold to hear the flocks bleat
For Reubens divisions looks searched in the heart   50
None breathed a word or a wish to retreat
Would Israel from God in her troubles depart

Gilead abode beyond Jordan away
Why did Dan in his ships on the ocean retire
On the seashore there Asher continued to stay
& abode in his breeches

But Zebulim Naphtali people of might
They jeoperded life unto Death on that day

CHILD HAROLD
[April – mid? May]

BIBLICAL PARAPHRASES
[April – mid? May]

In all the high places & field of the fight
They fought like the tiger devouring the prey   60

The Kings came & fought in the strength of his word
Kings of Canaan in Taanach arose like the sun
They took gain nor money in wars of the Lord
By the waters [of] Megiddo battled & won

Heaven fought in the cause whom the wicked disdain
The stars in their courses – the water & flood
All fought against Sisera – tempest & rain
& God drowned His anger in slaughter & blood

The old stream of Kishon it swept them away
That ancient of streams all its banks overflowed   70
O my soul thou hast trodden down strength on that day
For the strongest hearts quail in the strength of the Lord

The horse hoofs were broken with prancing & maimed
The prancings of mighty ones foiled in their toils
Their strength was exhausted their swiftness was lamed
& the Lord oer his people in victory smiles

Then the Angel of God in his vengance & ire
Uttered curses on Meroz & dwellers therein
Curse Meroz he said in a language of fire
Curse ye bitterly Meroz because of their sin   80

They fought not nor came to the help of the Lord
Where numbers & strength would his people oppose
To the Lord they would aid or assistance afford
When the pride of the mighty came down as their foes

But blessed be Jael & the kindred of Jael
Wife of Heber the Kenite whose courage was true

CHILD HAROLD
[April – mid? May]

BIBLICAL PARAPHRASES
[April – mid? May]

For blest above women – her heart did not fail
When the foe of the <   > lay <   >

He asked for water – she offered him milk
& brought him forth butter & bade him to eat   90
Sleep fell oer his weariness softer then silk
& eden seemed spreading her rest at his feet

But her hand she put forth to the hammer & nail
& pierced the proud head of her foe to the earth
At Her feet he bowed down & in death he turned pale
& lay like a shade without being or breath

The Mother of Sisera looked from her tower
& cried through the lattice 'Where, where can he stay
Why tarry the wheels of his chariots & power
Have they not sped & divided the prey   100

Her wise Ladies answered her eagerness – yea
She answered herself in the heaves of her heart
Have they not sped & divided the prey
To each man of spoils & of maidens a part

A prey of rich needlework took in the spoils
To Sisera the chief of the army – my son
A prey of rich colours rewarding the toils
& meet for the necks of the victors who won

Let all that love God be as bright as the sun
In the might of the morn & in goodness accord   110
Forty years the land rested when freedom was won –
So let all thine enemies perish O Lord

CHILD HAROLD
[mid? May – mid-July]

[mid? May – mid-July]

16

[Love?] is of heaven still the first akin
[Twas?] born in paradise & left its home
For desert lands stray hearts to nurse & win
Though pains like plagues pursue them where they roam
Its joys are ever green & blooms at home
The sailor rocking on the giddy mast   190
The soldier when the cannons cease to boom
& every heart its doubts or dangers past
Beats on its way for love & home at last

17

Nature thou truth of heaven if heaven be true
Falsehood may tell her ever changing lie
But natures truth looks green in every view
& love in every Landscape glads the eye
How beautiful these slopeing thickets lie
Woods on the hills & plains all smooth & even
Through which we see the ribboned evening skie   200
Though Winter here in floods & snows was driven
Spring came like God & turned it all to heaven

19

The Dew falls on the weed & on the flower
The rose & thistle bathe their heads in dew
The lowliest heart may have its prospering hour
The sadest bosom meet its wishes true

BIBLICAL PARAPHRASES
[mid? May – June]

[mid? May – June]

[Psalm 104: 20-6]

He harmonized darkness to night & repose
When the beast of the forest creep forth as our foes
After their prey the young Lions are roaring
Seeking meat from the God of all nature's adoring
They gather together at rise of the sun
& hide in their dens when his bounty is won
Man goeth to work as the morning sun smiles
& labours till eve brings release to his toils
How manifold Lord are thy works & thy power
Thou hast made all in wisdom both forest & flower   10
The earth it is full of thy riches & good
So is this great ocean & fathomless flood
Where small & great beasts of a wonderfull size
In numberless numbers our fancys surprise
Things creeping & swimming in harmonized strife
& there go the ships like to phantoms of life
& there's great leviathan spouting the spray
Which thou'st made in the depths of the ocean to play

Prayer of Habacuk

I heard thee O Lord & was stricken with fear
When the voice of thy wrath rung a knell to my ear
Revive thou thy work in the midst of my days
That my heart may rejoice in thy bounty & praise
O Lord ere thy vengance in fury come forth
Remember thy mercy in midst of thy wrath
Thou, Lord God of Temaan, thou most holy one

CHILD HAROLD

[mid? May – mid-July]

E'een I may joy love happiness renew
Though not the sweets of my first early days
When one sweet face was all the loves I knew
& my soul trembled on her eyes to gaze   210
Whose very censure seemed intended praise

20

A soul within the heart that loves the more
Giving to pains & fears eternal life
Burning the flesh till it consumes the core
So Love is still the eternal calm of strife
Thou soul within a soul thou life of life
Thou Essence of my hopes & fears & joys
M – y my dear first Love & early wife
& still the flower my inmost soul enjoys
Thy love's the bloom no canker worm destroys   220

21

Flow on my verse though barren thou mayest be
Of thought – Yet sing & let thy fancys roll
In Early days thou sweept a mighty sea
All calm in troublous deeps & spurned controul
Thou fire & iceberg to an aching soul
& still an angel in my gloomy way
Far better opiate then the draining bowl
Still sing my muse to drive cares fiends away
Nor heed what loitering listener hears the lay

BIBLICAL PARAPHRASES
[mid? May – June]

From the mountains of Paran thy presence was shown
Thy glory encircled the face of the sky
& the earth it was full of thy praise from on high   10
Thy brightness was glory the essence of light
& thy hands held the horns of thy power in my sight
Before thee pale famine & pestilence came
& coals at thy feet burnt & kindled to flame
He measured the earth in loud pealings of thunder
He beheld & the nations were driven asunder
The hills everlasting were shook in his scales
The perpetual mountains bowed down into vales
His power is eternal everlasting his ways
& earth air & heaven are full of his praise   20
The tents of all Cush in affliction I saw
& The Curtains of Midian did tremble in awe
Was thy wrath against rivers O Lord that they flee
Did thine anger swell mountains in calms of the sea
When thou rode on thy horses & chariots of fire
O Lord was the chosen's salvation thine Ire
Thy Bow was quite naked – Lord sheath up thy sword
According to the oaths of the tribes & thy word
Thou didst cleave earth with rivers that mightily sped
Mountains saw thee & trembled, yea, trembled & fled   30
Worlds of water broke loose & in thunder passed bye
The deep uttered voices & mounted on high
His brine in the clouds of the heaven was mixed
Sun & Moon in their grand habitation were fixed
These all wait on thee though high mountains in size
& their meat in due season thy bounty supplies
That thou givest they feed on as succour & food
Thou op'nest thy hand lo! it fills them with good
Thou hidest thy face they are troubled & cry
Thou takest their breath & in dust they all lie   40
Thou sendest thy spirit they start into birth
& again thou renewest the face of the earth

CHILD HAROLD
[mid? May – mid-July]

22

My themes be artless cots & happy plains 230
Though far from man my wayward fancies flee
Of fields & woods rehearse in willing strains
& I mayhap may feed on joys with thee
These cowslip fields this sward my pillow be
So I may sleep the sun into the west
My cot this awthorn hedge this spreading tree
– Mary & Martha once my daily guests
& still as mine both wedded loved & blest

23

I rest my wearied life in these sweet fields
Reflecting every smile in natures face 240
& much of joy this grass – These hedges yields
Not found in citys where crowds daily trace
Heart pleasures there hath no abideing place
The star gemmed early morn the silent even
[Sweet?] pleasures that our broken hopes deface
To love too well leaves nought to be forgiven
The Gates of Eden is the bounds of heaven

24 [7]

The apathy that fickle love wears through
The doubts & certaintys are still akin
Its every joy has sorrow in the view 250
Its holy truth like Eve's beguileing sin
Seems to be losses even while we win
Tormenting joys & cheating into wrong
& still we love – & fall into the Gin

BIBLICAL PARAPHRASES
[mid? May – June]

The glory of God is endureing for ever
The Lord shall rejoice in his works as the giver
Though thou lookest on earth & it quakes at thy stroke
Though he toucheth the hills in their pride & they smoke
I will sing while I live my creator to praise
I will sing praise to God to the end of my days
Meditation of him shall sweet comfort afford
& my heart shall be glad in the Love of the Lord   50
Let sinners consume from the face of the earth
Let the wicked no more have a being or birth
Bless thou the Lord o my heart & my soul
Praise ye the Lord long as seasons shall roll

[Numbers 23: 21-30]

In Jacob he hath not seen evil or guile
Nor in Israel perversness his truth to defile
Their Lord & their God these good tidings doth bring
& behold in their camps are the shouts of a king
God brought them from Egypt from bondage & ill
& he is as strong as a unicorn still
There is no enchantment can Jacob alarm
& Israel there's no divinations to harm
Of Jacob & Israel said it shall be
What hath God wrought that his people are free   10
Behold like a lion the people shall rise
& like a young lion the nations surprise
He shall not lie down till he eat of the prey
& drink of the blood of the slain in his way
Balak said unto Balaam I see they are free
Neither curse them nor bless them but hearken to me
Balaam answered Balak have I not swore
That what the Lord said I must do & no more?

CHILD HAROLD
[mid? May – mid-July]

My sun of love was short – & clouded long
& now its shadow fills a feeble song

Song

    I saw her in my springs young choice
    Ere loves hopes looked upon the crowd
    Ere loves first secrets found a voice
    Or dared to speak the name aloud   260

    I saw her in my boyish hours
    A Girl as fair as heaven above
    When all the world seemed strewn with flowers
    & every pulse & look was love

    I saw her when her heart was young
    I saw her when my heart was true
    When truth was all the themes I sung
    & Love the only muse I knew

    Ere infancy had left her brow
    I seemed to love her from her birth   270
    & thought her then as I do now
    The dearest angel upon earth

25

O she was more then fair – divinely fair
Can language paint the soul in those blue eyes
Can fancy read the feelings painted there
– Those hills of snow that on her bosom lies
Or beauty speak for all those sweet replies

BIBLICAL PARAPHRASES
[mid? May – June]

Then Balak to Balaam – come with me I pray thee
Peradventure 't'will please God to curse them for thee   20
Then he took him toward Jeshimon, to the top of mount peor
& build seven altars as wont' said the seer
Seven bullocks & rams for the Lord are requir'd
& Balak did all that the prophet desired

Balaams Parable Second Part[1]
Numbers Chap 24[b]

& when Balaam saw that it pleased the Lord well
To bless them – he sought not enchantment or spell
But he turned to the wilderness loved in his youth
Where nature & God live in silence & truth
& Balaam he cast up his eyes & again
Saw Israel abideing in tents on the plain
& the spirit of God came upon him like dew
& his parable then did the prophet pursue
Balaam hath said the offspring of Beor
& the man whose eyes have been open'd saith here   10
Who heard in the words of the Lord & who saw
Visions of th'almighty in tremblings & awe
Who fell in a trance but his eyes where unclosed
How goodly thy tents are O Jacob disposed
As beautifull valleys spread forth far & wide
As gardens like eden by th'rivers green side
As trees of lign aloes which God as the giver
Did plant – & as cedars beside the green river
He shall pour water out of his buckets – his seed
Shall be in the waters to flourish & speed   20
His king shall be higher then Agag in power
& his kingdom exalted in glory & dower
God brought him from Egypt – he hath as it were

CHILD HAROLD
[mid? May – mid-July]

That through loves visions like the sun is breaking
Wakeing new hopes & fears & stifled sighs
From first love's dreame's my love is scarcely waking   280
The wounds might heal but still the heart is aching

26

Her looks was like the spring her very voice
Was springs own music more then song to me
Choice of my boyhood nay my souls first choice
From her sweet thralldom I am never free
Yet here my prison is a spring to me
Past memories bloom like flowers where e'er I rove
My very bondage though in snares – is free
I love to stretch me in this shadey Grove
& muse upon the memories of love   290

3 [8]

Green bushes & green trees where fancy feeds
On the retireing solitudes of May
Where the sweet foliage like a volume reads
& weeds are gifts too choice to throw away
How sweet the evening now succeeds the day
The vevelt hillock forms a happy seat
The white thorn bushes bend with snowey may
Dwarf furze in golden blooms & violets sweet
Make this wild scene a pleasure grounds retreat

Hail Solitude still Peace & Lonely good
Thou spirit of all joys to be alone   300
My best of friends these glades & this green wood
Where nature is herself & loves her own

BIBLICAL PARAPHRASES
[mid? May – June]

The strength of a unicorn – terror & fear
Shall eat up the nations – his enemies all
Break their bones & with arrows pierced through they shall fall
He couched – he lay down as a lion at lair
As a great lion who shall compeat with him there
He whoso blesseth Gods people is blest
& cursed is he who shall injure their rest   30
Then Balak being wrath with the Seer of the Lord
Smote both hands together in anger unawed
Saying I called thee to curse them through nations & climes
& behold thou hast blessed them three seperate times
Now flee thee therefore to thy place from this hour
I thought to promote thee to honour & power
But thy God keeps thee back from all honours desert
So flye to his refuge & quickly depart
Then Balaam to Balak spoke fearless in thrall
Did I not say to thy messengers all
If Balak would let me his riches behold   40
& give me his house full of silver & gold
I cannot so wrong the commands of the Lord
To do good or ill of my feeble accord
But what the Lord showeth me that will I seek
& what my God biddeth me that will I speak
& now lo! I go to my people again
Come & I'll show thee – then language more plain
What this people here which my blessings must praise
Shall do to thy people in strifes latter days   50
& he took up his parable justly & clear
Saying Balaam the prophet the offspring of Beor
Who fell in a trance & yet having his eyes
Open to visions that gleamed in the skies
Do I not speak the most high in my voice
Are they not the almighty's his chosen & choice
I shall see him anon but not now with my eyes
& I shall behold him anon but not nigh

CHILD HAROLD
[mid? May – mid-July]

The hearts hid anguish here I make it known
& tell my troubles to the gentle wind
Friends cold neglects have froze my heart to stone
& wrecked the voyage of a quiet mind
With wives & friends & every hope disjoined

18⁹

Where are my friends & childern where are they
The childern of two mothers born in joy   310
One roof has held them – all have been at play
Beneath the pleasures of a mothers eye
– & are my late hope's blighted – need I sigh
Hath care commenced his long perpetual reign
The spring & summer hath with me gone bye
Hope views the bud a flower & not in vain
Long is the night that brings no morn again

Wrecked of all hopes save one to be alone
Where Solitude becomes my wedded mate
Sweet Forest with rich beauties overgrown   320
Where solitude is queen & riegns in state
Hid in green trees I hear the clapping gate
& voices calling to the rambling cows
I Laugh at Love & all its idle fate
The present hour is all my lot alows
An age of sorrow springs from lovers vows

Sweet is the song of Birds for that restores
The soul to harmony the mind to love
Tis natures song of freedom out of doors
Forests beneath free winds & clouds above   330

Out of Jacob a star shall illumine the skies
A Sceptre from Israel shall flourish & rise   60
& smite all the corners of moab with strife
& destroy all the childern of Sheth to the life
& Edom shall be a possesion & Seir
Shall be a possesion for enemies near
& Israel shall do valiant deed for their dower
Out of Jacob comes he with dominion & power
To destroy him that yet in the city remains
& prosper the freedom of mountains & plains
& when he had looked over Amaleck – he
Took up his parable justly & free   70
Amaleck first of all nations – the giver
Of life dooms thy end that thou perish forever
& he looked on the Kenites not caring to mock
Saying strong is thy place like a nest in the rock²
Nevertheless Kenites shall fail in that day
& Ashur shall carry them captives away
& he took up his parable – nothing to miss
Alas who shall live when my God doeth this
Ships come from Chittim in islet & river
T'afflict Ashur – & Ebor shall perish for ever   80
& Balaam arose to his place on that day
& Balak he also sojourned on his way

MISCELLANEOUS FRAGMENTS⁷

What happy thoughts the summer yields
Like woman soft & fair
The voice of Love is in the fields
While music fills the air

....

CHILD HAROLD
[mid? May – mid-July]

The Thrush & Nightingale & timid dove
Breathe music round me where the gipseys dwell –
Pierced hearts left burning in the doubts of love
Are desolate where crowds & citys dwell –
The splendid palace seems the gates of hell

MISCELLANEOUS FRAGMENTS
[mid? May – June]

– Truth must be truth & will where e'er we go
Though bigots howl & fight to answer 'No'

. . . .

Nigh Leopards hill stand All-ns hells
The public know the same
Where lady sods & buggers dwell
To play the dirty game

A man there is a prisoner there
Locked up from week to week
He's very fond they do declare
To play at hide & seek

With sweethearts so they seem to say
& such like sort of stuff   10
Well – one did come the other day
With half a pound of snuff

The snuff went here the snuff went there
& is not that a bad house
To cheat a prisoner of his fare
In a well ordered madhouse

They'll cheat you of your money friend
By takeing too much care o't
& if your wives their cun–ys send
They're sure to have a share o't   20

Now where this snuff could chance to stop
Perhaps gifts hurded are up
Till Mat & steward open shop
& have a jolly flare up

CHILD HAROLD
[June? – mid-July]

[June? – mid-July]

Many are poets – though they use no pen[10]
To show their labours to the shuffling age
Real poets must be truly honest men
Tied to no mongrel laws on flatterys page
No zeal have they for wrong or party rage   340
– The life of labour is a rural song
That hurts no cause – nor warfare tries to wage
Toil like the brook in music wears along –
Great little minds claim right to act the wrong

Ballad

Summer morning is risen
& to even it wends
& still Im in prison
Without any friends

I had joys assurance
Though in bondage I lie   350
– I am still left in durance
Unwilling to sigh

Still the forest is round me
Where the trees bloom in green
As if chains ne'er had bound me
Or cares had ne'er been

DON JUAN
[June? – mid-July]

Madhouses they must shut up shop
& tramp to fairs & races
Master & men as madmen stop
Life lives by changeing places

[June? – mid-July]

DON JUAN A POEM

"Poets are born" – & so are whores – the trade is
Grown universal – in these canting days
Women of fashion must of course be ladies
& whoreing is the business – that still pays
Playhouses Ball rooms – there the masquerade is
– To do what was of old – & now adays
Their maids – nay wives so innocent & blooming
Cuckold their spouses to seem honest women[8]

There's much said about love & more of women
I wish they were as modest as they seem   10
Some borrow husbands till their cheeks are blooming
Not like the red rose blush – but yellow cream
Lord what a while those good days are in coming –
Routs Masques & Balls – I wish they were a dream
– I wish for poor men luck – an honest praxis
Cheap food & cloathing – no corn laws or taxes

I wish – but there is little got bye wishing
I wish that bread & great coats ne'er had risen
I wish that there was some such word as 'pishun
For ryhme sake for my verses must be dizen   20
With dresses fine – as hooks with baits for fishing

CHILD HAROLD
[June? – mid-July]

Nature's love is eternal
In forest & plain
Her course is diurnal
To blossom again   360

For home & friends vanished
I have kindness not wrath
For in days care has banished
My heart possessed both

My hopes are all hopeless
My skys have no sun
Winter fell in youths mayday
& still freezes on

But Love like the seed is
In the heart of a flower   370
It will blossom with truth
In a prosperous hour

True love is eternal
For God is the giver
& love like the soul will
Endure – & forever

& he who studies natures volume through
& reads it with a pure unselfish mind
Will find Gods power all round in every view
As one bright vision of the almighty mind   380
His eyes are open though the world is blind
No ill from him creations works deform
The high & lofty one is great & kind
Evil may cause the blight & crushing storm
His is the sunny glory & the calm

DON JUAN
[June? – mid-July]

I wish all honest men were out of prison
I wish M.P's. would spin less yarn – nor doubt
But burn false bills & cross bad taxes out

I wish young married dames were not so frisky
Nor hide the ring to make believe they're single
I wish small beer was half as good as whiskey
& married dames with buggers would not mingle
There's some too cunning far & some too frisky
& here I want a ryhme – so write down "jingle"   30
& there's such putting in – in whores crim con
Some mouths would eat forever & eat on

Childern are fond of sucking sugar candy
& maids of sausages – larger the better
Shopmen are fond of good sigars & brandy
& I of blunt – & if you change the letter
To C or K it would be quite as handy
& throw the next away – but I'm your debtor
For modesty – yet wishing nought between us
I'd hawl close to a she as vulcan did to venus   40

I really cant tell what this poem will be
About – nor yet what trade I am to follow
I thought to buy old wigs – but that will kill me
With cold starvation – as they're beaten hollow[9]
Long speeches in a famine will not fill me
& madhouse traps still take me by the collar
So old wig bargains now must be forgotten
The oil that dressed them fine has made them rotten

I wish old wigs were done with ere they're mouldy
I wish – but heres the papers large & lusty   50
With speeches that full fifty times they've told ye
– Noble Lord John to sweet Miss Fanny Fusty[10]

CHILD HAROLD
[June? – mid-July]

Song

The sun has gone down with a veil on his brow
While I in the forest sit museing alone
The maiden has been oer the hills for her cow
While my hearts affections are freezing to stone
Sweet Mary I wish that the day was my own   390
To live in a cottage with beauty & thee
The past I will not as a mourner bemoan
For abscence leaves Mary still dearer to me

How sweet are the glooms of the midsummer even
Dark night in the bushes seems going to rest
& the bosom of Mary with fancys is heaving
Where my sorrows & feelings for seasons were blest
Nor will I repine though in love we're divided
She in the Lowlands & I in the glen
Of these forest beeches – by nature we're guided   400
& I shall find rest on her bosom agen

How soft the dew falls on the leaves of the beeches
How fresh the wild flower seems to slumber below
How sweet are the lessons that nature still teaches
For truth is her tidings wherever I go
From school days of boyhood her image was cherished
In manhood sweet Mary was fairer then flowers
Nor yet has her name or her memory perished
Though absence like winter oer happiness lowers

Though cares still will gather like clouds in my sky   410
Though hopes may grow hopeless & fetters recoil
While the sun of existance sheds light in my eye
I'll be free in a prison & cling to the soil
I'll cling to the spot where my first love was cherished
Where my heart nay my soul unto Mary I gave

DON JUAN
[June? – mid-July]

Is wed – a lie good reader I ne'er sold ye
– Prince Albert goes to Germany[11] & must he
Leave the queens snuff box where all fools are strumming
From addled eggs no chicken can be coming

Whigs strum state fiddle strings untill they snap
With cuckoo cuckold cuckoo year by year
The razor plays it on the barbers strap
– The sissars grinder thinks it rather quere   60
That labour wont afford him "one wee drap"
Of ale or gin or half & half or beer
– I wish prince Albert & the noble dastards
Who wed the wives – would get the noble bastards

I wish prince Albert on his german journey
I wish the Whigs were out of office &
Pickled in law books of some good atorney
For ways & speeches few can understand
They'll bless ye when in power – in prison scorn ye
& make a man rent his own house & land –   70
I wsh prince Alberts queen was undefiled
– & every man could get his *wife* with child

I wish the devil luck with all my heart
As I would any other honest body
His bad name passes bye me like a f – t
Stinking of brimstone – then like whisky toddy
We swallow sin which seems to warm the heart
– There's no imputing any sin to God – he
Fills hell with work – & is'n't it a hard case
To leave old whigs & give to hell the carcass   80

Me-b–ne may throw his wig to little Vicky[12]
& so resign his humbug & his power
& she with the young princess mount the dickey
On ass milk diet for her german tour[13]

CHILD HAROLD
[June? – mid-July]

& when my last hope & existance is perished
Her memory will shine like a sun on my grave

Mary thou ace of hearts thou muse of song
The pole star of my being & decay
Earths coward foes my shattered bark may wrong   420
Still thourt the sunrise of my natal day
Born to misfortunes – where no sheltering bay
Keeps off the tempest – wrecked where'eer I flee
I struggle with my fate – in trouble strong –
Mary thy name loved long still keeps me free
Till my lost life becomes a part of thee

Love is the main spring of existance – It
Becomes a soul wherebye I live to love
On all I see that dearest name is writ
Falsehood is here – but truth has life above   430
Where every star that shines exists in love
Skys vary in their clouds – the seasons vary
From heat to cold – change cannot constant prove
The south is bright – but smiles can act contrary
My guide star gilds the north – & shines with Mary

My life hath been one love – no blot it out
My life hath been one chain of contradictions
Madhouses Prisons wh-re shops – never doubt
But that my life hath had some strong convictions
That such was wrong – religion makes restrictions   440
I would have followed – but life turned a bubble
& clumb the jiant stile of maledictions
They took me from my wife & to save trouble
I wed again & made the error double

DON JUAN

[June? – mid-July]

Asses like ministers are rather tricky
I & the country proves it every hour
W-ll–gt-n & M-l—n in their station
Coblers to queens – are phisic to the nation

These batch of toadstools on this rotten tree
Shall be the cabinet of any queen   90
Though not such coblers as her servants be
They're of Gods making – that is plainly seen
Nor red nor green nor orange – they are free
To thrive & flourish as the Whigs have been
But come tomorrow – like the Whigs forgotten
You'll find them withered stinking dead & rotten

Death is an awfull thing it is by God
I've said so often & I think so now
Tis rather droll to see an old wig nod
Then doze & die the devil don't know how   100
Odd things are wearisome & this is odd –
Tis better work then kicking up a row
I'm weary of old Whigs & old whigs heirs
& long been sick of teazing God with prayers

I've never seen the cow turn to a bull
I've never seen the horse become an ass
I've never seen an old brawn cloathed in whool –
But I have seen full many a bonny lass
& wish I had one now beneath the cool
Of these high elms – Muse tell me where I was   110
O – talk of turning I've seen Whig & Tory
Turn imps of hell – & all for Englands glory

I love good fellowship & wit & punning
I love "true love" & God my taste defend
I hate most damnably all sorts of cunning –

CHILD HAROLD
[June? – mid-July]

Yet abscence claims them both & keeps them too
& locks me in a shop in spite of law
Among a low lived set & dirty crew
Here let the Muse oblivions curtain draw
& let man think – for God hath often saw
Things here too dirty for the light of day   450
For in a madhouse there exists no law –
Now stagnant grows my too refined clay
I envy birds their wings to flye away

How servile is the task to please alone
Though beauty woo & love inspire the song
Mere painted beauty with her heart of stone
Thinks the world worships while she flaunts along
The flower of sunshine butterflye of song
Give me the truth of heart in womans life
The love to cherish one – & do no wrong   460
To none – o peace of every care & strife
Is true love in an estimable wife

How beautifull this hill of fern swells on
So beautifull the chappel peeps between
The hornbeams – with its simple bell – alone
I wander here hid in a palace green
Mary is abscent – but the forest queen
Nature is with me – morning noon & gloaming
I write my poems in these paths unseen
& when among these brakes & beeches roaming   470
I sigh for truth & home & love & woman

I sigh for one & two – & still I sigh
For many are the whispers I have heard

DON JUAN
[June? – mid-July]

I love the Moor & Marsh & Ponders end –[14]
I do not like the song of "cease your funning"
I love a modest wife & trusty friend
– Bricklayers want lime as I want ryhme for fillups
– So here's a health to sweet Eliza Phillips[15]   120

Song

Eliza now the summer tells
Of spots where love & beauty dwells
Come & spend a day with me
Underneath the forest tree
Where the restless water flushes
Over mosses mounds & rushes
& where love & freedom dwells
With orchis flowers & fox glove bells
Come dear Eliza set me free
& oer the forest roam with me   130

Here I see the morning sun
Among the beachtree's shadows run
That into gold the short sward turns
Where each bright yellow blossom burns
With hues that would his beams out shine
Yet nought can match those smiles of thine
I try to find them all the day
But none are nigh when thou'rt away
Though flowers bloom now on every hill
Eliza is the fairest still   140

The sun wakes up the pleasant morn
& finds me lonely & forlorn
Then wears away to sunny noon
The flowers in bloom the birds in tune

CHILD HAROLD
[June? – mid-July]

From beautys lips – loves soul in many an eye
Hath pierced my heart with such intense regard
I Looked for joy & pain was the reward
I think of them I love each girl & boy
Babes of two mothers – on this velvet sward
& nature thinks – in her so sweet employ
While dews fall on each blossom weeping joy   480

Here is the chappel yard enclosed with pales
& oak trees nearly top its little bell
Here is the little bridge with guiding rail
That leads me on to many a pleasant dell
The fernowl chitters like a startled knell
To nature – yet tis sweet at evening still –
A pleasant road curves round the gentle swell
Where nature seems to have her own sweet will
Planting her beech & thorn about the sweet fern hill

I have had many loves – & seek no more –   490
These solitudes my last delights shall be
The leaf hid forest – & the lonely shore
Seem to my mind like beings that are free
Yet would I had some eye to smile on me
Some heart where I could make a happy home in
Sweet Susan that was wont my love to be
& Bessey of the glen – for I've been roaming
With both at morn & noon & dusky gloaming

Cares gather round I snap their chains in two
& smile in agony & laugh in tears   500
Like playing with a deadly serpent – who
Stings to the death – there is no room for fears

DON JUAN
[June? – mid-July]

While dull & dowie all the year
No smiles to see no voice to hear
I in this forest prison lie
With none to heed my silent sigh
& underneath this beachen tree
With none to sigh for Love but thee   150

Now this new poem is entirely new[16]
As wedding gowns or money from the mint
For all I know it is entirely true
For I would scorn to put a lie in print
– I scorn to lie for princes – so would you
& ere I shoot I try my pistol flint
– The cattle salesman – knows the way in trying
& feels his bullocks ere he thinks of buying

Lord bless me now the day is in the gloaming
& every evil thought is out of sight   160
How I should like to purchase some sweet woman
Or else creep in with my two wives to night –
Surely that wedding day is on the comeing
Abscence like phisic poisons all delight –
Mary & Martha both an evil omen
Though both my own – they still belong to no man

But to our text again – & pray where is it
Begin as parsons do at the beginning
Take the first line friend & you cannot miss it
"Poets are born" & so are whores for sinning   170
– Here's the court circular – o Lord is this it
Court cards like lists of —— not the naked meaning
Here's Albert going to germany they tell us
& the young queen down in the dumps & jealous

CHILD HAROLD
[June? – mid-July]

Where death would bring me happiness – his sheers
Kills cares that hiss to poison many a vein
The thought to be extinct my fate endears
Pale death the grand phis[i]cian cures all pain
The dead rest well – who lived for joys in vain

DON JUAN
[June? – mid-July]

Now have you seen a tramper on race courses
Seeking an honest penny as his trade is
Crying a list of all the running horses
& showing handbills of the sporting ladies
– In bills of fare you'll find a many courses
Yet all are innoscent as any maid is   180
Put these two dishes into one & dress it
& if there is a meaning – you may guess it

Don Juan was Ambassador from russia
But had no hand in any sort of tax
His orders hung like blossoms of the fushia
& made the ladies hearts to melt like wax
He knew Napoleon & the king of prusia
& blowed a cloud oer spirits wine or max
But all his profits turned out losses rather
To save one orphan which he forced to father   190

Theres Docter Bottle imp who deals in urine
A keeper of state prisons for the queen
As great a man as is the Doge of Turin
& save in London is but seldom seen
Yclep'd old A-ll-n – mad brained ladies curing
Some p-x-d like Flora & but seldom clean
The new road oer the forest is the right one
To see red hell & further on the white one[17]

Earth hells or b-gg-r sh-ps or what you please
Where men close prisoners are & women ravished   200
I've often seen such dirty sights as these
I've often seen good money spent & lavished
To keep bad houses up for docters fees
& I have known a b-gg-rs tally travers'd
Till all his good intents began to falter
– When death brought in his bill & left the halter

CHILD HAROLD
15 July

15 July

Written in a Thunder storm July 15ᵗʰ 1841[11]

The heavens are wrath – the thunders rattling peal
Rolls like a vast volcano in the sky
Yet nothing starts the apathy I feel   510
Nor chills with fear eternal destiny

My soul is apathy – a ruin vast
Time cannot clear the ruined mass away
My life is hell – the hopeless die is cast
& manhoods prime is premature decay

DON JUAN
[11 – 20? July]

O glorious constitution what a picking
Ye've had from your tax harvest & your tythe
Old hens which cluck about that fair young chicken
– Cocks without spurs that yet can crow so blythe   210
Truth is shut up in prison while ye're licking
The gold from off the gingerbread – be lythe
In winding that patched broken old state clock up
Playhouses open – but mad houses lock up

Give toil more pay where rank starvation lurches
& pay your debts & put your books to rights
Leave whores & playhouses & fill your churches
Old clovenfoot your dirty victory fights
Like theft he still on natures manor poaches
& holds his feasting on anothers rights   220
To show plain truth you act in bawdy farces
Men show their tools – & maids expose their arses

[11 – 20? July]

Now this day is the eleventh of July
& being sunday I will seek no flaw
In man or woman – but prepare to die
In two days more I may that ticket draw
& so may thousands more as well as I
To day is here – the next who ever saw
& In a madhouse I can find no mirth pay
– Next tuesday used to be Lord Byron's birthday[18]   230

Lord Byron poh – the man wot rites the werses
& is just what he is & nothing more
Who with his pen lies like the mist disperses
& makes all nothing as it was before

CHILD HAROLD
[20 – 23 July]

Roll on ye wrath of thunders – peal on peal
Till worlds are ruins & myself alone
Melt heart & soul cased in obdurate steel
Till I can feel that nature is my throne

I live in love sun of undying light   520
& fathom my own heart for ways of good
In its pure atmosphere day without night
Smiles on the plains the forest & the flood

Smile on ye elements of earth & sky
Or frown in thunders as ye frown on me
Bid earth & its delusions pass away
But leave the mind as its creator free

[20 – 23 July]

This twilight seems a veil of gause & mist[12]
Trees seem dark hills between the earth & sky
Winds sob awake & then a gusty hist   530
Fanns through the wheat like serpents gliding bye
I love to stretch my length 'tween earth & sky
& see the inky foliage oer me wave
Though shades are still my prison where I lie
Long use grows nature which I easy brave
& think how sweet cares rest within the grave

Life is to me a dream that never wakes
Night finds me on this lengthening road alone
Love is to me a thought that ever aches
A frost bound thought that freezes life to stone   540

DON JUAN
[11 – 20? July]

Who wed two wives & oft the truth rehearses
& might have had some twenty thousand more
Who has been dead so fools their lies are giving
& still in Allens madhouse caged & living

If I do wickedness to day being sunday
Can I by hearing prayers or singing psalms   240
Clear off all debts twixt god & man on monday
& lie like an old hull that dotage calms
& is there such a word as Abergundy
I've read that poem called the 'Isle of Palms'
– But singing sense pray tell me if I can
Live an old rogue & die an honest man

I wish I had a quire of foolscap paper
Hot pressed – & crowpens – how I could endite
A silver candlestick & green wax taper
Lord bless me what fine poems I would write   250
The very tailors they would read & caper
& mantua makers would be all delight
Though laurel wreaths my brows did ne'er environ
I think myself as great a bard as Byron

I have two wives & I should like to see them
Both by my side before another hour
If both are honest I should like to be them
For both are fair & bonny as a flower
& one o Lord – now do bring in the tea mem
Were bards pens steamers each of ten horse power   260
I could not bring her beautys fair to weather
So I've towed both in harbour blest together

Now i'n't this canto worth a single pound
From anybodys pocket who will buy
As thieves are worth a halter I'll be bound

CHILD HAROLD
[20 – 23 July]

Mary in truth & nature still my own
That warms the winter of my aching breast
Thy name is joy nor will I life bemoan –
Midnight when sleep takes charge of natures rest
Finds me awake & friendless – not distrest

Tie all my cares up in thy arms O sleep
& give my weary spirits peace & rest
I'm not an outlaw in this midnight deep
If prayers are offered from sweet womans breast
One & one only made my being blest   550
& fancy shapes her form in every dell
On that sweet bosom I've had hours of rest
Though now through years of abscence doomed to dwell
Day seems my night & night seems blackest hell

England my country though my setting sun
Sinks in the ocean gloom & dregs of life
My muse can sing my Marys heart was won
& joy was heaven when I called her wife
The only harbour in my days of strife
Was Mary when the sea roiled mountains high   560
When joy was lost & every sorrow rife
To her sweet bosom I was wont to flye
To undecieve by truth lifes treacherous agony

DON JUAN
[after? 23 July]

Now honest reader take the book & try
& if as I have said it is not found
I'll write a better canto bye & bye
So reader now the money till unlock it
& buy the book & help to fill my pocket   270

[after? 23 July]¹⁹

Milton sung Eden & the fall of man
Not woman for the name implies a wh—e
& they would make a ruin of his plan
Falling so often they can fall no lower
Tell me a worse delusion if you can
For innoscence — & I will sing no more
Wherever mischief is tis womans brewing
Created from manself — to be mans ruin

The flower in bud hides from the fading sun
& keeps the hue of beauty on its cheek   280
But when full blown they into riot run
The hue turns pale & lost each ruddy streak
So 't'is with woman who pretends to shun
Immodest actions which they inly seek
Night hides the wh—e — cupboards tart & pasty
Flora was p-x-d — & womans quite as nasty

Marriage is nothing but a driveling hoax
To please old codgers when they're turned of forty
I wed & left my wife like other folks
But not untill I found her false & faulty   290
O woman fair — the man must pay thy jokes
Such makes a husband very often naughty

CHILD HAROLD
23 – 24 July

23 – 24 July

Song a[13]

I've wandered many a weary mile
Love in my heart was burning
To seek a home in Mary[s] smile
But cold is loves returning
The cold ground was a feather bed
Truth never acts contrary
I had no home above my head   570
My home was love & Mary

I had no home in early youth
When my first love was thwarted
But if her heart still beats with truth
We'll never more be parted
& changing as her love may be
My own shall never vary
Nor night nor day I'm never free
– But sigh but abscent Mary

Nor night nor day nor sun nor shade   580
Week month nor rolling year
Repairs the breach wronged love hath made
There madness – misery here
Lifes lease was lengthened by her smiles
– Are truth & love contrary
No ray of hope my life beguiles
I've lost love home & Mary

DON JUAN
[after? 23 July]

Who falls in love will seek his own undoing
The road to marriage is – 'the road to ruin'

Love worse then debt or drink or any fate
It is the damnest smart of matrimony
A hell incarnate is a woman-mate
The knot is tied – & then we loose the honey
A wife is just the protetype to hate
Commons for stock & warrens for the coney   300
Are not more tresspassed over in rights plan
Then this incumberance on the rights of man

CHILD HAROLD
23 – 24 July

Song b

Here's were Mary loved to be
& here are flowers she planted
Here are books she loved to see   590
& here – the kiss she granted

Here on the wall with smileing brow
Her picture used to cheer me
Both walls & rooms are naked now
No Marys nigh to hear me

The church spire still attracts my eye
& leaves me broken hearted
Though grief hath worn their channels dry
I sigh oer days departed

The church yard where she used to play   600
My feet could wander hourly
My school walks there was every day
Where she made winter flowery

But where is angel Mary now
Loves secrets none disclose 'em
Her rosey cheek & broken vow
Live in my aching bosom

[late July – September]

Remind me not of other years or tell[14]
My broken hopes of joys they are to meet
While thy own falshood rings the loudest knell   610

BIBLICAL PARAPHRASES[20]
[August? – October?]

[August? – October?]

Davids Prayer

Who am I my God & my Lord
& what is my house in thy eye
Thou hast brought me here of thy sovereign accord
& cloathed me in majesty

CHILD HAROLD
[late July – September]

To one fond heart that aches too cold to beat
Mary how oft with fondness I repeat
That name alone to give my troubles rest
The very sound though bitter seemeth sweet –
In my loves home & thy own faithless breast
Truths bonds are broke & every nerve distrest

Friend of the friendless from a host of snares
From lying varlets & from friendly foes
I sought thy quiet truth to ease my cares
& on the blight of reason found repose   620
But when the strife of nature ceased her throes
& other hearts would beat for my return
I trusted fate to ease my world of woes
Seeking loves harbour – where I now sojourn
– But hell is heaven could I cease to mourn

For her for one whose very name is yet
My hell or heaven – & will ever be
Falsehood is doubt – but I can ne'er forget
Oaths virtuous falsehood volunteered to me
To make my soul new bonds which God made free   630
Gods gift is love & do I wrong the giver
To place affections wrong from Gods decree
– No when farewell upon my lips did quiver
& all seemed lost – I loved her more then ever

I loved her in all climes beneath the sun
Her name was like a jewel in my heart
Twas heavens own choice – & so Gods will be done
Love ties that keep unbroken cannot part

BIBLICAL PARAPHRASES
[August? – October?]

Yet this was a trifling thing unto thee
Thou hast spoke of thy servant whose house is to last
Like a man of estate & of noble degree
O God though in lowness his lot hath been cast

What can David speak more unto thee
For the honour of thy servant – or need   10
For thou knowest thy servant was of humble degree
& exaltest him highly indeed

O Lord for thy servants sake only
Hath thou done all this greatness to me
According to thy own heart thou blessed me once lonely
For all these great things are of thee

O Lord there is none beside thee
No other God living but thou
According to all that we hear or we see
From our beings beginning 'till now   20

There is no God but one – on the land or the sea
According to all we have heard with our ears
What nation is like to thy people now free
Israel redeemed of the Lord in their fears

God went to redeem them & make them a name
Of greatness & terribleness – even like thee
Driving out nations from before them like flame
The redeemed from proud Egypt – who conquered the sea

For Israel thy people thou madest thine own
& thou Lord became their own God e'en as mine   30
Let the thing thou hast spoke of thy servant be done
& his house be established forever as thine

CHILD HAROLD
[late July – September]

Nor can cold abscence sever or desert
That simple beauty blessed with matchless charms   640
Oceans have rolled between us – not to part
E'en Icelands snows true loves delirium warms
For there Ive dreamed – & Mary filled my arms

Song

O Mary sing thy songs to me
Of love & beautys melody
My sorrows sink beneath distress
My deepest griefs are sorrowless
So used to glooms & cares am I
My tearless troubles seem as joy
O Mary sing thy songs to me   650
Of love & beautys melody

"To be beloved is all I need
"& them I love are loved indeed"[15]
The soul of woman is my shrine
& Mary made my songs divine
O for that time that happy time
To hear thy sweet Piana's chime
In music so divine & clear
That woke my soul in heaven to hear

But heaven itself without thy face   660
To me would be no resting place
& though the world was one delight
No joy would live but in thy sight
The soul of woman is my shrine
Then Mary make those songs divine
For music love & melody
Breath all of thee & only thee

BIBLICAL PARAPHRASES
[August? – October?]

Do as thou hast said – be of goodness the giver
Let it even be established o Lord as thy will
That thy name may be magnified now & forever
& the true God be God of all Israel still

& a God to all Israel now & for aye
& the house of king David be established of thee
For thou o my God told thy servant that day
Thou wouldst build him a house – even so let it be   40

Therefore thy servant hath found in his heart
To pray before thee – & he knows from his soul
Thou art God & has promised thy love to impart
To thy servant as long as the seasons shall roll

The house of thy servant let it please thee to bless
That it may be before thee the boon & the giver
All nature & life doth thy bounty confess
& all that thou blesseth – is blessed & forever

Solomons Prayer &c &c

Then said Solomon the Lord hath made known
He would dwell in thick darkness with nature alone
But I've built an house where faith bows the knee
& built up a grand habitation for thee
& made thee a place for thy dwelling forever
There thy mercey may rest & thy love never sever
& the king turned his face & blessed while he turned
The whole congregation that hither sojourned
He blest them forever for God & his good
& the whole congregation of Israel stood   10
& he said blessed be God of Israel the Lord

CHILD HAROLD
[September – October?]

[September – October?]

Dull must that being live who sees unmoved[16]
The scenes & objects that his childhood knew
The school yard & the maid he early loved   670
The sunny wall where long the old Elms grew
The grass that e'en till noon retains the dew
Beneath the wallnut shade I see them still
Though not such fancys do I now pursue
Yet still the picture turns my bosom chill
& leaves a void – nor love nor hope may fill

After long abscence how the mind recalls
Pleasing associations of the past
Haunts of his youth – thorn hedges & old walls
& hollow trees that sheltered from the blast   680
& all that map of boyhood overcast
With glooms & wrongs & sorrows not his own
That oer his brow like the scathed lightening past
That turned his spring to winter & alone
Wrecked name & fame & all – to solitude unknown

So on he lives in glooms & living death
A shade like night forgetting & forgot
Insects that kindle in the springs young breath
Take hold of life & share a brighter lot
Then he the tennant of the hall & Cot   690
The princely palace too hath been his home
& Gipseys camp when friends would know him not
In midst of wealth a beggar still to roam
Parted from one whose heart was once his home

BIBLICAL PARAPHRASES
[August? – October?]

Who hath with his hands fullfilled his own word
That he spake unto David my father & said
"Since the day that I brought forth my people from dread
"From Egypt & bondage no city was named
"In the tribes of all Israel no dwelling proclaimed
"To build me an house that my name might be there
"Nor chose I a king for their comfort or care
"But my name now shall dwell in fair Jerusalem
"& David I've chosen as king over them"   20
Now it was in the heart of my father to raise
A house for the Lord whom all Israel should praise
But the Lord to my Father this thing did proclaim
As it was in thy heart to build an house to my name
As it was in thine heart to do so thou didst well
But thou shalt not build the house where my mercey shall dwell
Yet my mercey shall live & the thing shall be done
By the offspring that comes from thy loins & thy son
So the Lord hath performed all the words he hath spoken
& fulfilled all he vowed to my Father unbroken   30
For I'm set up as King upon Davids high throne
& have built up a house to Jehovah alone
& the ark of the covenant stands in its shade
Which God with the childern of Israel made
By the alter of God in thy presence Israel
He spread forth his hands in true worship & zeal
A scaffold of brass made King Solomon there
The height three cubits & five cubits square
In the midst of the court great Jehovah to please
& upon it he stood & then kneeled on his knees   40
Before the whole congregation whom God had forgiven
& spread forth his hands in the presence of heaven
& said O Lord God of all Israel – forgiven
There is no God like thee in the earth or the heaven
Who keepeth thy covenant truth as thy own
& still to thy servants thy mercey is shown

CHILD HAROLD
[September – October?]

& yet not parted – still loves hope illumes
& like the rainbow brightest in the storm
It looks for joy beyond the wreck of tombs
& in lifes winter keeps loves embers warm
The oceans roughest tempest meets a calm
Cares thickest cloud shall break in sunny joy   700
O'er the parched waste showers yet shall fall like balm
& she the soul of life for whom I sigh
Like flowers shall cheer me when the storm is bye

Now melancholly autumn comes anew[17]
With showery clouds & fields of wheat tanned brown
Along the meadow banks I peace pursue
& see the wild flowers gleaming up & down
Like sun & light – the ragworts golden crown
Mirrors like sunshine when sunbeams retire
& silver yarrow – there's the little town   710
& oer the meadows gleams that slender spire
Reminding me of one – & waking fond desire

I love thee nature in my inmost heart
Go where I will thy truth seems from above
Go where I will thy landscape forms a part
Of heaven – e'en these fens where wood nor grove
Are seen – their very nakedness I love
For one dwells nigh that secret hopes prefer
Above the race of women – like the dove
I mourn her abscence – fate that would deter   720
My hate for all things – strengthens love for her

BIBLICAL PARAPHRASES
[August? – October?]

While still they will walk with their whole hearts before thee
Thou who crownest David my Father with glory
Thou promised my Father & made it to stand
& spak'st with thy mouth & fullfilled with thy hand   50
Thou hast kept every promise nor took none away
But all are fullfilled as it is on this day
Now therefore God almighty of Israel the Lord
Still keep with David my father thy word
The promise thou made him saying that which is right
& there shall not fail thee a man in my sight
To sit over Israels great people & throne
So thy childern take heed to the law as my own
To walk in the way as I've laid before thee
In my law as thou hitherto hast before me   60
Now then God of Israel their being & Lord
Verifye that thou hast spoken – thy word
With David thy servant – O speak it agen
But will God in deed make his dwelling with men
On the earth will our prayers & petitions so gain thee
When the heaven of heavens hath not room to contain thee
How much less this temple which now I have built
Though the earth with thy love & thy glory is gilt
Therefore have respect to thy servant his prayer
Let not supplications be vapour & air   70
O Lord God almighty do list to the cry
Of thy servant who prays to his maker on high
Thou God of all Israel before thee I pray
That thy eyes may look over this house night & day
On the place of Jehovah the glory of fame
On the place thou hast chose as the house of thy name
& harken & heed as a symbol of grace
To the prayer which thy servant now prays to this place
Hear thou from thy dwelling place even in heaven
& hearing O Lord let our sins be forgiven   80
If a man sin against his neighbour – almighty forbear

CHILD HAROLD
[September – October?]

Song

Lovely Mary when we parted
I ne'er felt so lonely hearted
As I do now in field & glen
When hope says "we shall meet agen"
& by yon spire that points to heaven
Where my earliest vows was given
By each meadow field & fen
I'll love thee till we meet agen

True as the needle to the pole
My life I love thee heart & soul   730
Wa'n't thy love in my heart enrolled
Through love was fire 'twould soon be cold
By thy eyes of heavens own blue
My heart for thine was ever true
By sun & moon by sea & shore
My life I love thee more & more

& by that hope that lingers last
For heaven when lifes hell is past
By time the present – past & gone
I've loved thee – & I love thee on   740
Thy beauty made youths life divine
Till my soul grew a part of thine
Mary I mourn no pleasures gone –
The past hath made us both as one

That form from boyhood loved & still loved on[18]
That voice – that look – that face of one delight
Loves register for years, months, weeks – time past & gone
Her looks was ne'er forgot or out of sight
– Mary the muse of every song I write   750

BIBLICAL PARAPHRASES
[August? – October?]

& an oath be laid on him to make him to swear
& the oath to this house on thy alter they bring
Then hear thou from heaven & do the just thing
By requiteing the wicked doing justice to all
On his own head let the wickeds own reccompense fall
Justifying the righteous – his ways to approve
& giving his righteousness – mercey & love
If Israel get worse & from enemies flee
Because they have sinned against goodness & thee   90
& again shall confess thy great name & return
& make in this house supplication & mourn
Then hear thou from heaven & evil forgive
In Israel thy people that mercey may live
& bring them again like a wreck to the strand
To the place which thou gav'st them their fathers own land
When the heavens shut up have no season of rain
Because they have sinned against thee – once again
Yet if they turn toward this place & pray
& confess thy great name & return from their way   100
When thou dost afflict them – in mercey believe
Then hear thou from heaven o Lord & forgive
The sins of thy people & Israel shall know
The good way wherein thou hast taught them to go
On their land of inheritance scatter thy rain
& the land & thy people shall flourish again
If there be pestilence blastings & dearth
& mildews & locusts spreading deserts oer earth
If their enemies come & lay cities in thrall
& sickness & sores threaten death over all   110
Then what prayer soever by man shall be made
Or of thy people Israel when wronged & affraid
When every one knows his own grief to proclaim
& spreads forth his hands in this house to thy name
Then hear thou from heaven thy own dwelling place
& render to every man blessings & grace

CHILD HAROLD
[September – October?]

Thy cherished memory never leaves my own
Though cares chill winter doth my manhood blight
& freeze like Niobe my thoughts to stone –
Our lives are two – our end & aim is one

Song

They near read the heart
Who would read it in mine
That love can desert
The first truth on his shrine
Though in Lethe I steep it
& sorrows prefer   760
In my hearts core I keep it
& keep it for her

For her & her only
Through months & through years
I've wandered thus lonely
In sorrows & fears
My sorrows I smother
Though troubles anoy
In this world & no other
I cannot meet joy   770

No peace nor yet pleasure
Without her will stay
Life looses its treasure
When Mary's away
Though the nightingale often
In sorrow may sing
– Can the blast of the winter
Meet blooms of the spring

BIBLICAL PARAPHRASES
[August? – October?]

According to truth do thou raise them agen
For thou knowest the hearts of the childern of men
Which thou gave to our fathers our birthright to be –
That they may fear thee & walk in thy ways   120
So long as they live in the land of thy praise
Moreover conscerning the stranger with thee
Which is not of Israel but come from afar
For thy great name & justice in peace or in war
For thy hand that's almighty & outstr[et]ched arm
If they prey in this house – do thou keep them from harm
Then hear from the heavens thy dwelling on high
To the strangers petition do thou heed & reply
Though a stranger may plead do thou grant his request
That the people of earth may believe thee as best   130
As Israel doth know of thy goodness & fame
& may know that this temple is called by thy name
If thy people go out to thy enemies far
In the way that thy guideance shall send them to war
& their prayers unto thee towards this city proclaim
Towards the place & the house I have built for thy name
Then hear from the heavens – petitions & prayers
& mentain thy own cause in the peoples affairs
If they should sin against goodness & thee
For there is not a man that from sin is all free   140
& thou in thy anger sends strifes roughest waves
& deliver'st them up to their foemen as slaves
& they carry them captives in terror & fear
To lands & strange countrys far off or near
Yet should they bethink them whose childern they are
While they are captives & pray to thee there
In the midst of captivity saying aright
"That we have dealt wickedly Lord in thy sight"
If to thee they return with their soul & their heart
In the land of captivity – thither thou art   150
Although they are captives let them pray towards their land

CHILD HAROLD
[September – October?]

Thou first best & dearest
Though dwelling apart
To my heart still the nearest　　　　　　　　780
Forever thou art
& thou wilt be the dearest
Though our joys may be o'er
& to me thou art nearest
Though I meet thee no more

Song

Did I know where to meet thee
Thou dearest in life
How soon would I greet thee
My true love & wife　　　　　　　　790
How soon would I meet thee
At close of the day
Though cares would still cheat me
If Mary would meet me
I'd kiss her sweet beauty & love them away

& when evening discovers
The sun in the west
I long like true lovers
To lean on thy breast
To meet thee my dearest
– Thy eyes beaming blue　　　　　　　　800
Abscent pains the severest
Feel Mary's the dearest
& if Mary's abscent – how can I be true

How dull the glooms cover
This meadow & fen
Where I as a lover

BIBLICAL PARAPHRASES
[August? – October?]

& the citys to stay the dread wrath of thy hand
The land of their fathers great Lord & thy fame
& toward the house I have built for thy name
Then hear thou from heaven thy dwelling place – hear
Their prayers, supplications, & terrible fear
Forgive thy own people & dwell in their cause
& bring them once more to their land & thy laws
& though they have sinned before thee let them live
The erring restore before thee & – forgive   160
Let thine eyes Lord be open in mercey & grace
& attend to the prayer that is made in this place
Arise o Lord God in thy resting place – thou
Let thy priests o Lord God as before thee they bow
Be cloathed with salvation thy mercies to prove
& thy saints all rejoice in thy goodness & love
From th' face of thine anointed Lord turn not away
But remember the mercies of David for aye

Job – 38ᵗʰ Chap: 1ˢᵗ Part

Then God half angered ansered Job aright
Out of the wirlwind & the darkening storm
"Who darkeneth counsil thus & argues wrong
"By words without all knowledge vague & void
"Gird up thy loins now like a man – for I
"Demand of thee – & answer me aright
"Where wast thou mortal when I formed & laid
"Foundations of the earth & sea – declare
"If thou hast understanding think & speak
"Who hath the measures laid & knowest thou   10
"Or who hath stretched the line upon its base
"Whereon are earths foundations fastened – say
"Or who hath planned & laid the corner stone

CHILD HAROLD
[September – October?]

Seek Mary agen
But silence is teazing
Wherever I stray
There's nothing seems pleasing   810
Or aching thoughts easing
Though Mary live's near me – she seems far away

O would these gales murmur
My love in her ear
Or a birds note inform her
While I linger here
But nature contrary
Turns night into day
No bird – gale – or fairy   820
Can whisper to Mary
To tell her who seeks her – while Mary's away

This life is made of lying & grimace
This world is filled with whoring & decieving
Hypocrisy ne'er masks an honest face
Story's are told – but seeing is believing
& I've seen much from which there's no retrieving
I've seen deception take the place of truth
I've seen knaves flourish – & the country grieving
Lies was the current gospel in my youth   830
& now a man – I'm further off from truth

Fame blazed upon me like a comets glare
Fame waned left me like a fallen star
Because I told the evil what they are
& truth & falshood never wished to mar
My Life hath been a wreck – & I've gone far
For peace & truth – & hope – for home & rest

BIBLICAL PARAPHRASES
[August? – October?]

When all the morning stars together sang
& all the sons of God did shout for joy
Or who as if with doors shuts up the sea
When it break forth as issuing from the womb
When I made its garments of the racking clouds
& wrapt thick darkness as its swaddling bands
& brake up for it my decreed abode   20
& set up bars & doors to keep it staid
& said here shalt thou come not further
& here shalt thy proud waves be staid
Hast thou commanded morning since thy days
& caused the bright day spring to know its place
That it might hold on earths extreemest ends
& the wicked might be shaken out thereform
It is turned as clay into the seal
& they stand as garments cloathing it with light
Their light from wickedness is still withheld   30
& the high arm is broken in its might
Hast thou entered in the ocean springs
Or walked in search of the unfathomed deeps
Hath death his gates e'er opened unto thee
Or shown the shadows of eternal sleep
Hast thou perceived the breadth of earth or space
If thou knowest all or part thereof – declare
Where is the way wherein the light may dwell
& as for darkness where doth it repose
That thou should'st take it to the bound there of
& know the paths that leadeth to its home   40
Knowest thou as much because thou wast then born
Or since because thy numbered days was great
Hast thou entered the palace of the snow
Or hast thou seen the treasures of the hail
Which for the time of trouble I reserve
Against the day of battle & of war
By what way is light parted – knowest thou

CHILD HAROLD
[September – October?]

– Like Edens gates – fate throws a constant bar –
Thoughts may o'ertake the sunset in the west
– Man meets no home within a woman's breast   840

Though they are blazoned in the poets song
As all the comforts which our lifes contain
I read & sought such joys my whole life long
& found the best of poets sung in vain
But still I read & sighed & sued again
& lost no purpose where I had the will
I almost worshiped when my toils grew vain
Finding no antidote my pains to kill
I sigh a poet & a lover still

Thus saith the great & high & lofty one[19]   850
Whose name is holy – home eternity
In the high & holy place I dwell alone
& with them also that I wish to see
Of contrite humble spirits – from sin free
Who trembles at my word – & good receive
– Thou high & lofty one – O give to me
Truths low estate & I will glad believe
If such I am not – such I'm feign to live

Ballad[20]

Sweet days while God your blessings send
I call your joys my own   860
– & if I have an only friend
I am not left alone

She sees the fields the trees the spires
Which I can daily see

BIBLICAL PARAPHRASES
[August? – October?]

Which scattereth oer the earth the eastern wind
For the overflow of waters who divides   50
A channel & a course that it may speed
Who guides forked lightenings through the sultry sky
& gives the thunder terrors shuddering voice
To cause the rain on spots where no man is
On wildered wastes where no man cares to dwell
To satisfy the waste & desolate ground
& cause the bud to blossom there in spring
Hath the rain a father – silence – speak
Or who begets the drops of morning dew
Out of whose womb cometh the chilly ice   60
& the heavens hoar frost who gendered can[s]t thou tell
The waters are hidden as beneath a stone
& the face of the deep is frozen like a rock
The influences of Pleiades canst thou bind
Or loosen Orions belt – canst thou bring forth
Nazzaroth in his season or yet guide
Arcturus with his sons – man knowest thou
The ordinances of heaven – canst thou set
The dominion thereof in earth – let silence speak
Canst thou lift up thy voice to clouds & sky   70
& bid the rain in waters cover thee
Canst thou send lightenings forth that they may go
& answer 'here we are' – say who hath put
Wisdom in the inward parts & who hath given
Prime understanding to the beating heart
Who can number in wisdom heavens host of clouds
Or the bottles of heaven who can stay
When the clods cleave fast together & the dust
Groweth hard as a rock – can mortals hunt
Prey for the Lion or the lions whelps   80
When hid in dens or in the coverts couched
They lie in wait for prey – & who provides
The raven with his food – his young ones cry
To God & wander for the lack of meat

CHILD HAROLD
[September – October?]

& if true love her heart inspires
Life still has joys for me

She sees the wild flower in the dells
That in my rambles shine
The sky that oer her homstead dwells
Looks sunny over mine   870

The cloud that passes where she dwells
In less then half an hour
Darkens around these orchard dells
Or melts a sudden shower

The wind that leaves the sunny south
& fans the orchard tree
Might steal the kisses from her mouth
& waft her voice to me

O when will autumn bring the news
Now harvest browns the fen   880
That Mary as my vagrant muse
& I shall meet agen

Tis pleasant now days hours begin to pass
To dewy Eve – To walk down narrow close
& feel ones feet among refreshing grass
& hear the insects in their home discourse
& startled blackbird flye from covert close
Of white thorn hedge with wild fears fluttering wings
& see the spire & hear the clock toll hoarse
& whisper names – & think oer many things   890
That love hurds up in truths imaginings

BIBLICAL PARAPHRASES
[August? – October?]

The New Jerusalem Rev. Chap 21ˢᵗ

& I looked & I saw a new heaven
& earth on the bosom of day
For the first earth was fled with its deeds unforgiven
& its heaven had perished away
& the ocean was dry & no longer it ran
Which had rolled ever since the creation of man

& I John the most holy city descried
New Jerusalem coming for God to the living
Adorned for her husband prepared as a bride
& I heard a great voice speaking loud from the heaven   10
Behold the tabernacle of God is with men
& there he will dwell with his people agen

They shall be his people united & free
The choice of his love not the fear of his rod
& God shall dwell with them forever & be
Their soul keeping saviour redeemer & God
He shall wipe away all the tears from their eyes   .
There shall be no more death neither sorrows nor crys

Nor shall there be any more sickness or pain
For the world & their sickness is passed & away   20
& he that sat on the throne said again
In language as bright as meridian day
& he said to me write I make all things as new
& the words which I spake are both faithfull & true

& once more he said unto me – now it is done
I am Alpha – Omega – beginning & end
Their thirst shall have water as clear as the sun
For I am lifes fountain benefactor & friend
To him that oercometh all goodness is won
His God I will be then & he is my son   30

CHILD HAROLD
[September – October?]

Song

Dying gales of sweet even
How can you sigh so
Though the sweet day is leaving
& the sun sinketh low
How can you sigh so
For the wild flower is gay
& her dew gems all glow
For the abscence of day

Dying gales of sweet even
Breath music from toil   900
Dusky eve is loves heaven
& meets beautys smile
Love leans on the stile
Where the rustic brooks flow
Dying gales all the while
How can you sigh so

Dying gales round a prison
To fancy may sigh
But day here hath risen   910
Over prospects of joy
Here Mary would toy
When the sun it got low
Even gales whisper joy
& never sigh so

Labour lets man his brother
Retire to his rest
The babe meets its mother
& sleeps on her breast –
The sun in the west   920
Has gone down in the ocean

BIBLICAL PARAPHRASES
[August? – October?]

But the vain unbelieving & them that have fear
The abominable – murderers whoremongers & liars
Idolaters scorcerers mocking the seer
I leave in the lake of unquenchable fires
There burning forever their being & breath
& this is the second existance of death

One of the seven angels then came unto me
Which held the seven plagues in seven phials of strife
Saying come hither & I will show unto thee
The light of salvation the bride & lambs wife   40
& me in the spirit he carried away & won
To a great & high mountain that peered to the sun

Whose forhead looked green in the realms of the sky
Whose crags in the beams of eternity nod
& shewed me a city great glorious & high
New Jerusalem descending from heaven & God
Having Gods glory eternitys light
As precious as jasper as crystal more bright

& had a great wall shining spacious & high
& twelve gates about it that glittered like flames   50
& twelve angels watched from the realms of the sky
& written thereon were the tribes & their names
On the east & the north six gates I descried
& the south & the west three on every side

Twelve foundations the walls of the city upheld
& twelve names thereon – the apostles of God
& he that talked with me a golden reed held
An emblem of justice & truth not his rod
To measure the city the gates & the wall
In kindness & love doing equal by all   60

CHILD HAROLD
[September – October?]

Dying gales gently sweep
O'er the hearts ruffled motion
& sing it to sleep

Song

The spring may forget that he reigns in the sky
& winter again hide her flowers in the snow
The summer may thirst when her fountains are dry
But I'll think of Mary wherever I go
The bird may forget that her nest is begun
When the snow settles white on the new budding tree   930
& nature in tempests forget the bright sun
But I'll ne'er forget her – that was plighted to me

How could I – how should I – that loved her so early
Forget – when I've sung of her beauty in song
How could I forget – what I've worshiped so dearly
From boyhood to manhood – & all my life long –
As leaves to the branches in summer comes duly
& blossoms will bloom on the stalk & the tree
To her beauty I'll cling – & I'll love her as truly
& think of sweet Mary wherever I be   940

Song

No single hour can stand for nought
No moment hand can move
But calenders a aching thought
Of my first lonely love

BIBLICAL PARAPHRASES
[August? – October?]

& the plan of the city it lieth foursquare
The breadth is as long as the height & the length
Twelve thousand furlongs his reed measured there
The contents of that city of glory & strength
The length & the breadth & the height of the plan
Are equal – like God in his mercey to man

& he measured the wall with the reed in his hand
Of cubits one hundred & forty & four
According to the measure of a man was the wand
That is of the angel who guarded the door   70
The walls was of jasper the city pure gold
As clear as a mirror of glass to behold

The walls of the city were garnished like fire
With all manner of sorts of rich precious stones
The first foundation was jasper the second sapphire
The third chalcedony more splendid then thrones
The fourth was an emerald green as the waves
Of the earth that was vanished with oceans & graves

The fifth was sardonix & sardius the sixth
The seventh was chrysolyte – yellow & green   80
& Beryl the eight[h] & of yellow unmixt
The ninth was a topaz – the rest they were seen
Chrysoparsus a jacinth an amethist – blue
As violets that in the old fallen world grew

The twelve gates were twelve pearls of delight to behold
Every gate was one pearl where no mortal could look
& the street of the city was paved with pure gold
Transparent as glass & the waves of a brook
& no temple there showed itself in my sight
For the Lord God himself was its temple & light   90

CHILD HAROLD
[September – October?]

Where silence doth the loudest call
My secrets to betray
As moonlight holds the night in thrall
As suns reveal the day

I hide it in the silent shades
Till silence finds a tongue   950
I make its grave where time invades
Till time becomes a song

I bid my foolish heart be still
But hopes will not be chid
My heart will beat – & burn – & chill
First love will not be hid

When summer ceases to be green
& winter bare & blea –
Death may forget what I have been
But I must cease to be   960

When words refuse before the crowd
My Marys name to give
The muse in silence sings aloud
& there my love will live

Now harvest smiles embrowning all the plain
The sun of heaven oer its ripeness shines
"Peace–plenty" has been sung nor sung in vain
As all bring forth the makers grand designs
– Like gold that brightens in some hidden mines
His nature is the wealth that brings increase   970
To all the world – his sun forever shines
– He hides his face & troubles they increase
He smiles – the sun looks out in wealth & peace

BIBLICAL PARAPHRASES
[August? – October?]

No need had the city of sun or the moon
To shine on its splendour – the builder & giver
Of its glory – was also its light & its boon
His sun shone upon it for ever & ever
There the nations of them that are saved meet a home
There the kings of the earth bring their glories & come

& its gates they shall never be closed by day
& night in that city shall never be known
The righteous shall there truth & glory display
& the honour of nations shall make it their own   100
No wickedness here shall destroy their abode
Or enemies poison the friendship of God

In no wise shall enter any thing to defile
& no abomination of evil come nigh
No wickedness working deception or guile
Nor any that forgeth or maketh a lie
But they which are written in Gods book of life
They shall live here forever from sorrow & strife

The River of the Water of Life –
Rev. Chap. 22

& he showed me a river in midst of the street
Of the water of life clear as chrystal & pure
Flowing out from the throne of the Lord – heaven sweet
The weary to bless & the feeble to cure
& on each side the river like comfort in thrall
The tree of life grew as a blessing for all

CHILD HAROLD
[September – October?]

Song[21]

O Mary dear three springs have been
Three summers too have blossomed here
Three blasting winters crept between
Though abscence is the most severe
Another summer blooms in green
But Mary never once was seen

I've sought her in the fields & flowers   980
I've sought her in the forest groves
In avanues & shaded bowers
& every scene that Mary loves
E'en round her home I seek her here
But Marys abscent every where

Tis autumn & the rustling corn
Goes loaded on the creaking wain
I seek her in the early morn
But cannot meet her face again
Sweet Mary she is abscent still   990
& much I fear she ever will

The autumn morn looks mellow as the fruit[22]
& ripe as harvest – every field & farm
Is full of health & toil – yet never mute
With rustic mirth & peace the day is warm
The village maid with gleans upon her arm
Brown as the hazel nut from field to field
Goes cheerily – the valleys native charm –
I seek for charms that autumn best can yield
In mellowing wood & time ybleaching field   1000

BIBLICAL PARAPHRASES
[August? – October?]

Twelve manner of fruits did its branches supply
That every month ripened – so fertile the sod
& the leaves of the tree 'neath Jehovahs own eye
Held a cure for the nations who trusted in God   10
No curse shall there be in that endless of day
With the Lord – where his servants shall serve him for aye

& his name it shall be on their forheads of light
& they shall see his face – nor his majesty shun
No candle is needed where never was night
Neither is wanted the light of the sun
For the Lord God of light & of life is the giver
& they shall reign with him forever & ever

& he said unto me all these sayings are true
& faithfull – & now are as being begun   20
The God of the prophets sent his angel to shew
To his servants the things which must shortly be done
Behold I come quickly & blessed is he
Who keepeth the sayings of this prophecy

I John saw these things & heard while I saw
& when I had heard & had seen unforgot
I fell at the feet of the angel with awe
But he said unto me see thou do it not
For I'm thy fellow servant & worship aright
& of my bretheren the prophets who live in his light   30

Of them which keep the sayings this book doth contain
Of which thou art witness what God doth reveal
Worship God – him alone – other worship is vain
These sayings he said unto me – never seal
Leave the prophecy open till all understand
For the kingdom is come & the time is at hand

CHILD HAROLD
[September – October?]

Song

Tis autumn now & natures scenes
The pleachy fields & yellowing trees
Looses their blooming hues & greens
But nature finds no change in me
The fading woods the russet grange
The hues of nature may desert
But nought in me shall find a change
To wrong the angel of my heart
For Mary is my angel still
Through every month & every ill   1010

The leaves they loosen from the branch
& fall upon the gusty wind
But my hearts silent love is staunch
& nought can tear her from my mind
The flowers are gone from dell & bower
Though crowds from summers lap was given
But love is an eternal flower
Like purple amaranths in heaven
To Mary first my heart did bow
& if she's true she keeps it now   1020

Just as the summer keeps the flower
Which spring conscealed in hoods of gold
Or unripe harvest met the shower
& made earths blessings manifold
Just so my Mary lives for me
A silent thought for months & years
The world may live in revellry
Her name my lonely quiet cheers
& cheer it will what e'er may be
While Mary lives to think of me   1030

BIBLICAL PARAPHRASES
[August? – October?]

& he that's unjust – unjust let him be
& he that is filthy live filthy at will
& he that is righteous – leave righteousness free
& he that is holy live holily still   40
Behold I come quickly my reward is with me
To give all men according as his work it shall be

I am Alpha Omega beginning & end
Time past as the present – the first & the last
They are blest that on all my commandments attend
The tree of life is their right – when lifes troubles is past
The gates are all open the passage is free
& the new golden city their dwelling shall be

For without the dogs growl & the sorcerers cheat
& murder that stabs with idolators bye   50
& whoremongers all their old deeds to repeat
& they whoso loveth & maketh a lie
I Jesus have sent my angel t'record
These things unto you & the church of the Lord

I am the offspring of David & root
& I am the bright & the morning star
& the bride & the spirit say come – eat the fruit
& let him that heareth say come from afar
& let him that parcheth with thirst come & drink
For the water of life ever flows to the brink   60

To every man living I now testify
That hears the words of this book – & yet doeth the sin
To add any thing unto this prophecy
God shall send him the plagues that are written therein
& if any man take from this book – dealing strife
God shall take out his part from the volume of life

CHILD HAROLD

[September – October?]

Sweet comes the misty mornings in september
Among the dewy paths how sweet to stray
Greensward or stubbles as I well remember
I once have done – the mist curls thick & grey
As cottage smoke – like net work on the sprey
Or seeded grass the cobweb draperies run
Beaded with pearls of dew at early day
& oer the pleachy stubbles peeps the sun
The lamp of day when that of night is done

What mellowness these harvest days unfold   1040
In the strong glances of the midday sun
The homesteads very grass seems changed to gold
The light in golden shadows seems to run
& tinges every spray it rests upon
With that rich harvest hue of sunny joy
Nature lifes sweet companion cheers alone –
The hare starts up before the shepherd boy
& partridge conveys wir on russet wings of joy

The meadow flags now rustle bleached & dank
& misted oer with down as fine as dew   1050
The sloe & dewberry shine along the bank
Where weeds in blooms luxuriance lately grew
Red rose the sun & up the morehen flew
From bank to bank the meadow arches stride
Where foamy floods in winter tumbles through
& spread a restless ocean foaming wide
Where now the cowboys sleep nor fear the coming tide

About the medows now I love to sit
On banks bridge walls & rails as when a boy

BIBLICAL PARAPHRASES
[August? – October?]

& in the most holy city shall meet with no home
Nor share of the things in this volume of joy
He that testifieth this saitheth quickly I come
Even so come Lord Jesus all sin to destroy   70
The power of Gods love be with all – now – & then
& the grace of christ jesus be with you – Amen

*The Last Judgment – St Matt. from
Ver. 31ª to the end*

When the son of man comes in his glory anew
& all holy angels surrounding him too
Then shall he sit upon glory his throne
& before him all nations be gathered as one

The one from the other he'll seperate then
The wise & the good from lascevious men
The sheep from the goats the good shepherds divide
As gold in the furnace is heated & tried

When his sheep are no longer of comfort bereft
Shall be placed on his right hand & the goats on his left   10
Come ye blessed of God bid to troubles adieu
& inherit the kingdom prepared for you

From the foundation of earth – the beginning of time
Come of every colour from every clime
For when I was hungered ye offered me meat
& when I was thirsty your water was sweet

Ye lodged me a stranger – forsaken of all
When naked ye cloathed me nor left me in thrall

CHILD HAROLD
[September – October?]

To see old trees bend oer the flaggy pit   1060
With hugh roots bare that time does not destroy
Where sits the angler at his days employ
& there Ivy leaves the bank to climb
The tree – & now how sweet to weary joy
– Aye nothing seems so happy & sublime
As sabbath bells & their delightfull chime

Sweet solitude thou partner of my life[23]
Thou balm of hope & every pressing care
Thou soothing silence oer the noise of strife
These meadow flats & trees – the autumn air   1070
Mellows my heart to harmony – I bear
Lifes burthen happily – these fenny dells
Seem Eden in this sabbath rest from care
My heart with loves first early memory swells
To hear the music of those village bells

For in that hamlet lives my rising sun
Whose beams hath cheered me all my lorn life long
My heart to nature there was early won
For she was natures self – & still my song
Is her through sun & shade through right & wrong   1080
On her my memory forever dwells
The flower of Eden – evergreen of song
Truth in my heart the same love story tells
– I love the music of those village bells

Song

Heres a health unto thee bonny lassie o
Leave the thorn o' care wi' me

BIBLICAL PARAPHRASES
[August? – October?]

I was in prison ye came to me there
& your talk made my bonds unconfined as the air   20

Then shall the righteous say when did we Lord
See thee an hungered & offer thee food
Or thirsty to give thee of drink as a guest
A stranger to find thee a welcome & rest

Or naked & cloathed thee in part of our wealth
When saw we thee sick & restored thee to health
Or in prison came to thee to make thy bonds free
& the king shall make answer – ye did it to me

For verily I say unto you in as much
As ye've done it to the least of my brothers twas such   30
Ye have done it to me in the mind & the heart –
He shall say to the left now ye cursed depart

From me into hell everlasting & fire
With the devils own tortures & never expire
For I was an hungered & ye gave me no meat
& athirst but ye brought me no drink in my heat

I was a stranger ye offered no rest
Naked ye cloathed me not – sick & distrest
Ye visited not to give health or set free
Then shall they say Lord – whenever did we   40

See then an hungered or sick or athirst
Or naked or stranger or in bonds from the first
& did not administer comfort to thee
Then shall he answer them saying – as ye

Did it not to the poorest & least of my fold
Your friendship to me was as barren & cold

CHILD HAROLD
[September – October?]

& whatever I may be
Here's happiness to thee
Bonny lassie o

Here's joy unto thee bonny lassie o   1090
Though we never meet again
I well can bear the pain
If happiness is thine
Bonny lassie o

Here is true love unto thee bonny lassie o
Though abscence cold is ours
The spring will come wi' flowers
& love will wait for thee
Bonny lassie o

So heres love unto thee bonny lassie o   1100
Aye wherever I may be
Here's a double health to thee
Till life shall cease to love
Bonny lassie o

The blackbird startles from the homestead hedge[24]
Raindrops & leaves fall yellow as he springs
Such images are natures sweetest pledge
To me there's music in his rustling wings
"Prink prink" he cries & loud the robin sings
The small hawk like a shot drops from the sky   1110
Close to my feet for mice & creeping things
Then swift as thought again he suthers bye
& hides among the clouds from the pursueing eye

BIBLICAL PARAPHRASES
[August? – October?]

& these shall go away to the punishment due
But the righteous shall find joys eternity true

Lamentations of Jeremiah
Chap. 3

I am the man that affliction hath seen
By the rod of his wrath sorely scourged have I been
He hath turned against me like a vision of night
& led me to darkness & not into light
He turneth his hand against me all the day
My flesh & my skin he made old as a prey
He hath builded against me & broken my bones
I'm compassed with gall & travel & moans
He hath set me in places of darkness & cold
Like a being forgot as the dead are of old   10
He hath made my chain heavy & hedged me about
He hath shut out my prayer & I cannot get out
He hath enclosed all my ways with hewn heavy stone
& made all my paths both crooked & lone
He was unto me as a bear by the way
Or hiding in secret as a lion to slay
He pulled me in pieces my ways were all turned
Like a desolate being I sorrowed & mourned
I'm a mark for his arrow he bendeth his bow
& empties his quiver to pince me with woe   20
To my people I was a derision & prey
& their song was my sufferings all the long day
He hath filled me with bitterness trouble & thrall
& made me mad drunk both with wormwood & gall
With gravel stones also my teeth he hath broke
He hath covered me over with ashes & smoke
Thou took my souls peace in a desolate hour

CHILD HAROLD
[September – October?]

BIBLICAL PARAPHRASES
[August? – October?]

I forgot my prosperity riches & power
& I said that my strength in the Lord now must sever
& my hopes in my God now are perished forever   30
Remembering mine afflictions my misery & thrall
Confinement persecution – the wormwood & gall
My soul hath them still in remembrance the pain
& is humbled within me to feel it again
This I recall to my mind & I sigh
Yet therefore have hope that the worst may be bye
It is of Gods mercies we are not consumed
Because his compasssions fail not – yet entombed
His love seems to me in the desolate hours
Yet faith shall be new every morning like flowers   40
The Lord saith my soul is my portion & stay
Therefore he's my hope both by night & by day
The Lord he is good unto them that will wait
To the soul that will seek him both early & late
It is good that a man he should hope without friends
For the Lord of salvation to make him amends
It is good that a man bear the yoke of his youth
& endure persecution for the sake of the truth
He keepeth his silence & sitteth alone
Because he hath born it as a grief of his own   50
He hideth & putteth his mouth in the dust
If so that the Lord be his hope & his trust
He giveth his cheek to the smiter nor fears
He is filled with reproach at their insolent jeers
For his Lord & his God forsake him will never
& though he cause grief will not leave him for ever
He will have compassion – I am not affraid
For his mercies in multitudes come to our aid
He hurteth not willingly th'afflicted agen
Nor willingly grieveth the childern of men   60
To c[r]ush underfoot the imprisoned of earth
To turn aside the right of a man from his birth

CHILD HAROLD
[September – October?]

BIBLICAL PARAPHRASES
[August? – October?]

To subvert a man in his cause or to blot
But his right the most high he approveth it not
Who saith & it cometh to pass in the sun
When the Lord he commandeth it not to be done
Out of Gods mouth it was ne'er understood
That mixture proceeded of evil & good
Wherefore doth a living man daily complain
When our sins they are punished rebukeing is vain   70
Let us search out our ways & to comfort accord
& turn us agen to the help of the Lord
Let us lift up our hearts & our hands unforgiven
Imploreing God the most high & the mercies of heaven
We have transgressed & rebelled against thee
Thou hast covered with anger – persecuted we flee
Thou hast not pardoned we seek thee again
Thou hast not pittied but smitten & slain
Thou hast covered thyself in the depth of a cloud
That our prayer should not pass or be heard uttered loud   80
In the midst of thy people – the great & the small
Thou hast made us the refuse offscouring of all
All enemies open their mouths to deride
Fear & snares are against us on every side
Desolation destruction hath left us no shore
With rivers of waters mine eyes runneth oer
For the destruction of the daughter of my people's renown
Without intermission my tears trickle down
Till the lord shall look down from the heavens & see
I mourn for my own citys daughters & me   90
Mine enemies chased like a bird from its nest
My heart from its home & would give me no rest
They've cut off my life in the dungeon – to sever
& cast a stone on the door of my freedom forever
I said I'm cut off & my heart it felt dead
When waters & darkness flowed over mine head
From out the low dungeon I called on thy name

CHILD HAROLD
[September – October?]

BIBLICAL PARAPHRASES
[August? – October?]

Thou heardest O Lord my petition & came
Hide not thine ear to my breathing & cry
Thou drawest near in the day that I thought I should die   100
'Fear not' was the voice when I called upon thee
Thou hast pleaded the cause of my soul & I'm free
Thou hast witnessed my wrongs & redeemed my life
Judge thou my cause thou hast witnessed the strife
Against me all their vengance thy wisdom hath seen
& thou knowest what their hidden immag[in]ings mean
The lips of all those who rose up in the fray
Their device against me is as clear as the day
Their reproaches thou hearest – when they sit down or rise
I am their music to scoff & despise   110
Render them Lord as their justice demands
A reccompence mete to the work of their hands
Give them sorrow of heart that may inly condemn
Be the hatred of heaven thy curse upon them
Persecute & destroy them as somthing abhored
From under the face of thy heaven O Lord

Job Chap. 39

Knowest thou the time when wild goats breed
On rocks – or mark when the swift hinds calve
Canst thou number the months that they fulfill
Or know the time when they bring forth their young
They bow themselves in travail & bring forth
& cast out their fond sorrows on the hills
Their young ones are the image of themselves
They grow up with corn go forth & not return
Who hath sent out the wild ass free or who
Hath loosed his weary bonds – whose house I made   10
The wilderness – his home the barren land

CHILD HAROLD
[September – October?]

BIBLICAL PARAPHRASES
[August? – October?]

The multitudes of citys are his scorn
Neither regardeth he the drivers cry
His free born pasture is the mountain range
His search is after every thing thats green
Will Unicorns thy slaving voice obey
Or by thy crib abide – or in the glebe
Bind him to trace the furrow – or will he
Harrow the fertile valley after thee
Wilt thou trust him because his strength is great   20
Or wilt thou leave thy labour to his will
Wilt thou trust him to garner up thy seed
& gather home thine harvest to the barn
Gavest thou the peacocks tail his purple gold
Or wings & feathers to the ostrich tribe
Who leaveth her eggs on the earth to hatch
Warming them in the dust – forgetting that
The foot may crush or wild beast break their shells
Against her young ones she is hard & strange
As though they were not hers – her labour is   30
In vain withouten fear – God hath deprived
Her heart of reason – understanding lacks
To aid her toils – yet when she soars on high
She scorns both horse & rider in her flight
Hast thou given the horse his strength or cloathed
His neck with thunder – canst thou make him fear
& flee like a grasshopper – the glory
Of his nostrils is fierce & terrible
He paweth the ground in strength rejoiceing
& goeth onward to meet the battle
He scorns to be affraid & mocks at fear   40
Neither turneth he away from the sword
Against him the loaded quiver rattles
The glittering spear & the burnished shield
& his untamed fierceness swallows the ground
Neither heeds he the sound of the trumpet

104

CHILD HAROLD
[October – November]

[October – November]

The lightenings vivid flashes – rend the cloud[25]
That rides like castled crags along the sky
& splinters them to fragments – while aloud
The thunders heavens artillery vollies bye
Trees crash, earth trembles – beast[s] prepare to flye
Almighty what a crash – yet man is free
& walks unhurt while danger seems so nigh –
Heavens archway now the rainbow seems to be
That spans the eternal round of earth & sky & sea

1120

MISCELLANEOUS FRAGMENTS
[October? – November?]

He drives among the trumpets & laugheth ah ah
& the rage of battle he smelleth afar
The thunder of captains & shoutings of war
Doth thy weak wisdom teach the hawk to flye   50
& stretch her wings toward the southern sky
At thy command doth eagles mount & make
Their nests on high – their erie is the rock
In the strong place & on the rocky crag
From thence their prey is noted & their eyes
Beholdeth far – her young ones suck up blood
& where the slain is – there the eagles flye

MISCELLANEOUS FRAGMENTS[17]

[October? – November?]

So let us all be jolly
& laugh off melancholly
For grieving is a folly
Within the life of man
Then push about the joram
Leave the glass of joy before 'em
& mirth make up the quorum
We'll be happy if we can

....

CHILD HAROLD
[October – November]

A shock, a moment, in the wrath of God
Is long as hell's eternity to all
His thunderbolts leave life but as the clod
Cold & inna[ni]mate – their temples fall
Beneath his frown to ashes – the eternal pall
Of wrath sleeps oer the ruins where they fell
& nought of memory may their creeds recall
The sin of Sodom was a moments yell   1130
Fires death bed theirs their first grave the last hell

The towering willow with its pliant boughs
Sweeps its grey foliage to the autumn wind
The level grounds where oft a group of cows
Huddled together close – or propped behind
An hedge or hovel ruminate & find
The peace – as walks & health & I pursue
For natures every place is still resigned
To happiness – new life's in every view
& here I comfort seek & early joys renew   1140

The lake that held a mirror to the sun
Now curves with wrinkles in the stillest place
The autumn wind sounds hollow as a gun
& water stands in every swampy place
Yet in these fens peace harmony & grace
The attributes of nature are alied
The barge with naked mast in sheltered place
Beside the brig close to the bank is tied
While small waves plashes by its bulky side

BIBLICAL PARAPHRASES
[October? – November]

My heart my dear Mary from thee cannot part
[space left for a second line]
But the sweetest of pleasure that joy can impart
Is nought to the memory of thee

. . . .

His face is like a dragon
His a-se is like a frog
At heart a mere piegon
In manner quite a hog

BIBLICAL PARAPHRASES[22]

[October? – November]

Job Chap 40

Moreover God answered Job & said
Shall he who contends with God instruct him
He that reproveth God – let man reprove
Then Job made answer Lord behold I'm vile
What shall I answer thee – my voice is dumb
I lay my hand upon my mouth & fear
Once have I spoken but I answer not
Nay twice – nor further dare I now proceed
Then out of the fierce whirlwind & the storm
The Lord he answered fearfull Job & spake   10
"Gird up thy loins again & like a man –
I will demand of thee – declare & speak

CHILD HAROLD
[October – November]

BIBLICAL PARAPHRASES
[October? – November]

Wilt thou my judgments disannul & me
Condemn as wrong – that thou mayst righteous be
Is thine the power – hast thou an arm like God
Or canst thou thunder with a voice like him
Thyself with excellence & majesty array
With glory & with beauty deck thyself
& cast abroad thy rage of viewless ire
Behold the proud abase him with thy wrath –   20
Around look on the proud & bring him low
Tread underfoot the wicked in their place
Together hide them in degrading dust
& bind their faces under secret thralls
Then will I also unto thee confess
That thy right hand & arm thy self can save
Behold Behemoth which I made with thee
He eateth grass as doth the ox – lo now
His strength is in his loins his force & power
Is in the navel of his belly – moving now   30
His tail like to a cedar – his sinewed stones
Are wrapt together – his bones are strong as brass
Aye firm unflinching all as iron bars
Chief of Gods ways is he – he that made him
Can make his sword to pierce him & destroy
The mountains surely bring him forth his food
Where all the beast o' th' field do herd & play
Coverts of shady trees do make his lair
In the reed forests of the untrodden fens
The shady trees doth cover him with shadow   40
& willow brooks encompass him with shade
Behold he drinks a river in his thirst
& trusts to swallow Jordan in his mouth
He takes it with his eyes in thirsty draughts
& his nose pierces through the hidden snares

CHILD HAROLD
[October – November]

BIBLICAL PARAPHRASES
[October? – November]

Job 41 Chap

Canst thou with hooks Leviathan draw out
Or with a chord let down amidst the deep
Canst thou put hooks into his mountain nose
Or bore his jaw through with a feeble thorn
Will he to thee a supplication make
Or speak soft words to make a friend of thee
Will he with thee make covenant – or thou
Make him for aye thy servant or thy slave
Wilt thou as with a bird play with his strength
Or bind him for thy maidens sportive smiles
Shall thy companions banquet on his flesh   10
Or part him among merchants for rich gain
Or canst thou fill his skin with barbed hooks
Or pierce his island of a head with spears
Lay thy hand on him & the battle fear
Remember thou the strife & do no more
Thy hopes of him behold are all in vain
Shall not *one* at his sight be soon cast down
To stir him up theres none so fierce to dare
Who then is able by my power to stand   20
Who hath prevented that I should repay
All under the whole heavens lives as mine
His parts & powers I will not consceal
His great proportions & his jiant powers
The facing of his garment who can see
Or with his double bridle tamper *him*
The doors of his face who can unlock
His teeth stand round as terrible as death
His scales they are his pride shut up secure
From mortal eye as is a closed seal   30
One to another joins the common air
Comes not between them – nor a passage finds
They stick & join & sundering is in vain

CHILD HAROLD
[October – November]

BIBLICAL PARAPHRASES
[October? – November]

He [s]neeses & a splendid light doth shine
His eyes are like the mornings bright & fair
Out of his mouth breath comes like burning lamps
& issuing sparks leap out as living fire
His nostrils as a boiling chaldron smokes
His breath is kindled coals – & terrors flames
Come issuing from his mouth in terrors play   40
In's neck like to a mountain strength remains
& sorrow before him is turned to joy
His flakes of flesh join firm within themselves
& fast as is the mountain cant be moved
His heart is like the stone of adamant
Nay as the nether millstone firm & hard
When he is roiled the mighty are affraid
When he breaks forth they purifye themselves
The sword assailing him will never hold   50
The dark harbergeon or glittering spear
Iron is straw & brass as rotten wood
The arrow neither makes him fear or flee
Sling stones are stubble aiming at his power
Darts count as rotten straw & are no more
He laugheth at the shaking of a spear
Sharp stones are under him he heeds them not
He spreads sharp pointed things upon the mire
The sea beneath him like a chaldron boils
& like a pot of oil or ointment shines
& after him a path of light shines far   60
One thinks the sea all hoary where he swims
Earth owns nought like him made within a fear
High things are open to his mountain view
King over all the childern brutes of pride

CHILD HAROLD
[October – November]

BIBLICAL PARAPHRASES
[October? – November]

Peterborough rhyming version[23]

Canot thou draw out Leveathon
With an hook or a chord
Which thou lettest down
– Like the breath of a word

Canst thou put a hook in his nose
Or bore through his jaw with a thorn
Will he supplicate unto thee
Man to him is as mist in the morn

Unto thee will he speak in soft words
Or a covenant make up with thee   10
To him seas scarce a lodging affords
Wilt thou take him thy servant to be

Wilt thou play with his strength as a bird
Or bind him thy maidens to please
Shall thy friends make a banquet of him
That monarch & king of the seas

Shall they sell him to merchants for gain
Whose life like an island moves on
Canst thou fill his head with fish spears on the main
Do but strike & thy strength it is gone   20

Lay on him thine hand do no more
Remember the battle & strife
Behold him thy hope is no more
The sight of him dangers thy life

None are so fierce that dare stir him to strife
This monster & king of the sea

[November]

Song[26]

The floods come oer the meadow leas   1150
The dykes are full & brimming
Field furrows reach the horses knees
Where wild ducks oft are swimming
The skyes are black the fields are bare
The trees their coats are loosing
The leaves are dancing in the air
The sun its warmth refusing

Brown are the flags & fadeing sedge
& tanned the meadow plains
Bright yellow is the osier hedge   1160
Beside the brimming drains
The crows sit on the willow tree
The lake is full below
But still the dullest thing I see
Is self that wanders slow

The dullest scenes are not so dull
As thoughts I cannot tell
The brimming dykes are not so full
As my hearts silent swell
I leave my troubles to the winds   1170
With none to share a part
The only joy my feeling finds
Hides in an aching heart

BIBLICAL PARAPHRASES
[October? – November]

Then how can a man the mere shadow of life
Be able to stand before me

Who hath served me with the justice & truth
That I should repay him with favours divine   30
Whatsoever exists upon earth & in sooth
The whole that the heavens containeth are mine

Psalm 19

The heavens his wonderous works declare
The firmament his power
His handyworks are written there
Through every day & hour

Day unto day in language speaks
Night unto night will shine
In knowledge – & all language reads
& hears that voice divine

Their line & words through all the earth
Hath all the world oer run   10
His tabernacle there hath birth
A dwelling for the sun

As a bridegroom from his chamber comes
He shows his shineing face
Rejoiceing as the season blooms
As a strong man runs a race

His going forth is from the end
& to the end of heaven
His circuit shines on every land
Where his rays of life are given   20

CHILD HAROLD
[November]

Abscence in love is worse then any fate
Summer is winters desert & the spring
Is like a ruined city desolate
Joy dies & hope retires on feeble wing
Nature sinks heedless – birds unheeded sing
Tis solitude in citys – crowds all move
Like living death – though all to life still cling   1180
The strongest bitterest thing that life can prove
Is womans undisguise of hate & love

Song

I think of thee at early day
& wonder where my love can be
& when the evening shadows grey
O how I think of thee

Along the meadow banks I rove
& down the flaggy fen
& hope my first & early love
To meet thee once agen   1190

I think of thee at dewy morn
& at the sunny noon
& walks with thee – now left forlorn
Beneath the silent moon

I think of thee I think of all
How blest we both have been –
The sun looks pale upon the wall
& autumn shuts the scene

BIBLICAL PARAPHRASES
[October? – November]

The law of God a perfect law
Converts the soul & tries
Gods testimonies all are pure
& makes the simple wise

The statutes of the Lord are sure
The heart rejoiceing still
The Lords comandments they are pure
My eyes with love they fill

The fear of God is clean & pure
Endureing still forever   30
The judgments of the Lord are sure
& righteous as the giver

& more to be desired are they
Then gold can e'er become
More sweeter then the honey jar
Or e'en the honeycomb

Their stedfast truth thy servant warms
Their faith is his regard
In keeping them my being earns
A safe & sure reward   40

Who can his errors understand
Cleanse me from secret faults
Keep back thy servant in thy hands
That he nor fails nor halts

Let no presumtious sins e'er have
Dominion over me
Then shall I meet a welcome grave
Or live upright with thee

CHILD HAROLD
[November]

I can't expect to meet thee now
The winter floods begin   1200
The wind sighs throug[h] the naked bough
Sad as my heart within

I think of thee the seasons through
In spring when flowers I see
In winters lorn & naked view
I think of only thee

While life breaths on this earthly ball
What e'er my lot may be
Wether in freedom or in thrall
Mary I think of thee   1210

Song

Thourt dearest to my bosom
As thou wilt ever be
While the meadows wear a blossom
Or a leaf is on the tree
I can forget thee never
While the meadow grass is green
While the flood rolls down the river
Thou art still my bonny queen

While the winter swells the fountain
While the spring awakes the bee   1220
While the chamois loves the mountain
Thou'lt be ever dear to me
Dear as summer to the sun
As spring is to the bee
Thy love was soon as won
& so twill ever be

MISCELLANEOUS
11 November

Of vile transgressions great & small
Lord keep me innoscent   50
Then shalt thou hear my conscience call
& know my good intent

The meditations of my heart
Lord keep them all with thee
Let all the words my thoughts impart
With thy own sanction be

Do thou accept me e'er I fall
By thy avenging rod
My strength my hope my life my all
& my redeeming God   60

MISCELLANEOUS

11 November

Tis martinmass from rig to rig
Ploughed fields & meadow lands are blea
In hedge & field each restless twig
Is dancing on the naked tree
Flags in the dykes are bleached & brown
Docks by its sides are dry & dead
All but the ivy bows are brown
Upon each leaning dotterels head

Crimsoned with awes the awthorns bend
Oer meadow dykes & rising floods
The wild geese seek the reedy fen   10

CHILD HAROLD
[mid-November – December]

Thou'rt loves eternal summer
The dearest maid I prove
With bosom white as ivory
& warm as virgin love   1230
No falsehood gets between us
Theres nought the tie can sever
As cupid dwells with venus
Thou'rt my own love forever

[mid-November – December]

Tis winter & the fields are bare & waste[27]
The air one mass of "vapour clouds & storms"
The suns broad beams are buried & oercast
& chilly glooms the midday light deforms
Yet comfort now the social bosom warms
Friendship of nature which I hourly prove   1240
Even in this winter scene of frost & storms
Bare fields the frozen lake & leafless grove
Are natures grand religion & true love

Song[28]

In this cold world without a home
Disconsolate I go
The summer looks as cold to me
As winters frost & snow
Though winters scenes are dull & drear
A colder lot I prove
No home had I through all the year   1250
But Marys honest love

123

BIBLICAL PARAPHRASES
[mid-November – December]

& dark the storm comes oer the woods
The crowds of lapwings load the air
With buzes of a thousand wings
There flocks of starnels too repair
When morning oer the valley springs

BIBLICAL PARAPHRASES

[mid-November – December]

Psalm 91

He that dwelleth in the secret place
Of God the great & high
Beneath the shadow of his grace
In quiet peace shall lie

The Lord my lasting friend shall be
He is my refuge still
The fortress of my cares is he
& trust in God I will

Surely from the fowlers snare
He shall deliver thee   10
& from the noisesome pestilence
Still keep thee pure & free

His truth shall shield & buckler give
When hell its vengance flings
Beneath his feathers thou shalt live
& his defending wings

CHILD HAROLD
[mid-November – December]

But Love inconstant as the wind
Soon shifts another way
No other home my heart can find
Life wasting day by day
I sigh & sit & sit & sigh
For better days to come
For Mary was my hope & joy
Her truth & heart my home

Her truth & heart was once my home   1260
& May was all the year
But now through seasons as I roam
Tis winter everywhere
Hopeless I go through care & toil
No friend I e'er possest
To reccompence for Marys smile
& the love within her breast

My love was ne'er so blest as when
It mingled with her own
Told often to be told agen   1270
& every feeling known
But now loves hopes are all bereft
A lonely man I roam
& absent Mary long hath left
My heart without a home

BIBLICAL PARAPHRASES
[mid-November – December]

Nights terrors all shall flee away
Nor fears thy soul alarm
The arrows that are shot by day
Shall do thy life no harm   20

From pestilence that walks by night
Thy dwelling shall be free
Distruction that at noon shall blight
Shall never injure thee

A thousand by thy side shall fall
Ten thousand by thy hand
But nought shall bring thee into thrall
While God thy friend shall stand

Thou shalt behold it with thine eyes
The wicked's sure reward   30
Because the Lord thy refuge lies
Thy house is Gods regard

No evil thou shalt meet at large
No plague thy dwelling rase
For he shall give his angels charge
To keep thee all thy days

Thee they shall bear up in their hands
Nor leave thee all alone
Lest thou should'st dash in troubles lands
Thy foot against a stone   40

Thou shalt tread on the Lions main
& crush the adders crown
Young Lions by thy foot be slain
That tramples Dragons down

CHILD HAROLD
[mid-November – December]

BIBLICAL PARAPHRASES
[mid-November – December]

Because on me he sets his love
I'll keep his heart from shame
I'll set him high all foes above
Because he knows my name

On me his inward love shall call
In care I'll bring relief   50
I'll answer him in every thrall
& honour his belief

With length of life & honours too
Him I will satisfye
To him salvation will I shew
When troubles days are bye

Psalm 97

The earth reigneth now earth is green in his smiles
Let gladness extend through her hundreds of isles
Clouds & darkness are round him almighty & lone
& truths righteous judgments inhabit his throne
A fire goes before him that never burns out
That burns up his enemies round & about
His thunders & lightenings blazon the world
The earth saw & trembled where ruin was hurled
Where the Lord of the earth in his majesty sped
Hills melted like wax in his presence & fled   10
The heavens his righteousness prove every hour
& all people see both his glory & power
Worship him all ye Gods & confounded be they
Who serve graven images beings of clay
Zion saw & was glad at the voice of his word
Judahs Daughters rejoiced in thy judgments O Lord

CHILD HAROLD
[mid-November – December]

BIBLICAL PARAPHRASES
[mid-November – December]

The Lord oer the earth is exalted & high
For above all the Gods is his home in the sky
Hate evil ye people whose love is the Lord
He preserveth his saints by the truth of his word   20
He delivereth from evil & bondage & thrall
From the hand of the wicked he saveth them all
For the righteous the light of his mercey is sown
To the up right of heart all his gladness is shown
Ye righteous rejoice in the Lord all your days
To the memory of his holiness offer your praise

[Psalm 102: 1-17]

Lord hear my prayer when trouble glooms
Let sorrow find a way
& when the day of trouble comes
Turn not thy face away
My bones like hearth stones burn away
My life like vapoury smoke decays

My heart is smitten like the grass
That withered lies & dead
& I so lost to what I was
Forget to eat my bread   10
My voice is groaning all the day
My bones prick through this skin of clay

The wildernesses pelican
The deserts lonely owl
I am their like a desert man
In ways as lone & foul
As sparrows on the cottage top
I wait till I with faintness drop

CHILD HAROLD
[mid-November – December]

BIBLICAL PARAPHRASES
[mid-November – December]

I bear my enemies reproach
All silently I mourn   20
They on my private peace encroach
Against me they are sworn
Ashes as bread my trouble shares
& mix my food with weeping cares

Yet not for them is sorrows toil
I fear no mortals frown
But thou hast held me up awhile
& thou hast cast me down
My days like shadows waste from view
I mourn like withered grass in dew   30

But thou Lord shalt endure forever
All generations through
Thou shalt to Zion be the giver
Of joy & mercy too
Her very stones are in their trust
Thy servants reverence her dust

Heathens shall hear & fear thy name
All kings of earth thy glory know
When thou shalt build up Zions fame
& live in glory there below   40
He'll not despise their prayers though mute
But still regard the destitute

Isaiah Chap 47[24]

Come down & sit in dust
Daughter of Babalon
Come on the ground ye must

CHILD HAROLD
[mid-November – December]

BIBLICAL PARAPHRASES
[mid-November – December]

Thy throne & power is gone
Daughter of the chaldeans thy race is oer
Thou art the tender & delicate no more

Take millstones & grind meal
Uncover thy fair locks
Bare legs & thighs reveal
For God thy treachery mocks   10
Pass oer the streams thy nakedness is seen
& shame is oer thee though thou art a queen

Thy inmost shame is seen
Reverse thy every plan
I'll vengance take nor mean
To meet thee as a man
As for our redeemer he feels shame
The holy one of Israel is his name

Sit there in silence now
& into darkness flye   20
Uncoronet thy brow
Chaldeans daughter sigh
For thou shalt never more be called
Lady of kingdoms thy base power enthralled

I with my people wrath
Did their heritage polute
& in thine hands left both
To make them destitute
Thou shewed no mercey but with heavy stroke
Upon the ancient hast thou laid the yoke   30

I'm a Lady & forever
Thou saidst it – so depart
Thou remembered not the giver

CHILD HAROLD
[mid-November – December]

BIBLICAL PARAPHRASES
[mid-November – December]

Nor laid these things to heart
No wickedness on earth can thee defend
Thou ne'er remembered once the latter end

Therefore hear thou this
Thou Lady to pleasures given
That dwelleth careless & amiss
& rests no hope on heaven   40
Saying "I am" as there was none beside
"& know no loss of childern in my pride"

"Nor be a widow lone"
Yet these too mournfull things
Shall in a moment reach thy throne
With all that sorrow brings
For all thy devinations shall they come
& leave thy pomp all childless & no home

In wickedness thy trust
Hath said none seeth me   50
Thy wisdom & thy lust
It hath perverted thee
& thou hast said & felt it in thy heart
There's none beside me – sorsoress depart

Therefore shall evil come
From whence thou shalt not know
All powerless thou to shun the doom
Or to avert the blow
To sudden desolation shalt thou go
& to the ruin which thou shalt not know   60

With thy enchantments stand
That ever against the truth
The labours of thy sceptered hand

CHILD HAROLD
[mid-November – December]

BIBLICAL PARAPHRASES
[mid-November – December]

& even known from youth
If profit springs from each liscentious tale
If so be thou with wickedness prevail

With many counsils now
Thou'rt weak & weary grown
Astrollogers may bow
Around thy tottering throne   70
Stargazers soothsayers let them save or shun thee
From things that surely now shall come upon thee

Behold as stubble they
Before the fire shall burn
Themselves shall pass away
& know not where to turn
They shall not deliver themselves from the power
Of the flame which shall ignite consume & devour

In that desolate charm
There shall not be a fire   80
Or a coal left to warm
Though through cold they expire
Thus shall they be unto thee & ungrieved
With whom thou hast laboured & revelled & lived

Thy merchants from thy youth
They shall wander one & all
To his quarters & the truth
Shall leave thee more in thrall
Though slave dealers take thee though bondsmen enslave thee
There's none shall be able to shield thee or save thee   90

THE PROSE OF 1841

17 March[1]

Leppits Hill March 17th 1841

My Dear Wife Patty

   It Make's Me More Than Happy To Hear That You & My Dear Family Are All Well – And You Will All Be As Well Pleased To Hear That I Have Been So Long In Good Health & Spirits As To Have Forgotten That I Ever Was Any Otherways – My Situation Here Has Been Even From The Beginning More Then Irksome But I Shake Hands With Misfortune & Wear Through The Storm – The Spring Smile's & So Shall I – But Not While I Am Here – I Am Very Happy To Hear My Dear Boy Mention His 'Brother's & Sister's' So Kindly As I Feel Assured That They Love One Another As They Have Ever Done – It Was My Lot To Seem As Living Without Friends Untill I Met With You & Though We Are Now Parted My Affection Is Unaltered – & We Shall Meet Again I Would Sooner Wear The Trouble's Of Life Away Single Handed Then Share Them With Others – As Soon As I Get Relieved On Duty Here I Shall Be In Northamptonshire – Though Essex Is A Very Pleasant County – Yet To Me 'There Is No Place Like Home' – As My Childern Are All Well – To Keep Them So Besure & Keep Them In Good Company & Then They Will Not Only Be Well But Happy – For What Reason They Keep Me Here I Cannot Tell For I Have Been No Otherways Than Well A Couple Of Year's At The Least & Never Was Very Ill Only Harrassed By Perpetual Bother – & It Would Seem By Keeping Me Here One Year After Another That I Was Destined For The Same Fate Agen & I Would Sooner Be Packed In A Slave Ship For Affrica Then Belong To The Destiny Of Mock Friends & Real Enemies – Honest Men & Modest Women Are My Friends

   Give My Best Love To My Dear Childern & Kiss The Little One's For Me   Good Bye & God Be With You All Forever

   I Had Three Seperate Dream's About Three Of My Boys Or Your

PROSE
17 March, 11–12 April

Boys – Frederick John & William – Not Any Ways Remarkable Only I
Was In A Wreck With The Latter – Such Things Never Trouble Me Now
In Fact Nothing Troubles Me & Thank God It Is So – I Hope The Time
Is Not Long Ere I Shall See You All By Your Own Fireside Though
Every Day In Abscence Seem's To Me Longer Then Year's
    I Am My Dear Wife Your Affectionate Husband
                         John Clare

P.S. Give My Love To The Dear Boy Who Wrote To Me & To Her
Who Is Never Forgotten
                   God Bless You All   J. Clare

To Martha Turner Clare
Northborough / Northamptonshire / Near Market Deeping

11–12 April

Note for Child Harold[2]

Easter Sunday – 1841   Went In The Morning To Buckhurst Hill Church
& Stood In The Church Yard – When A Very Interesting Boy Came Out
While Organ Was Playing Dressed In A Slop Frock Like A Ploughboy &
Seemingly About Nine Years Of Age   He Was Just Like My Son Bill
When He Was About The Same Age & As Stout Made – He Had A
Serious Interesting Face & Looked As Weary With The Working Days As
A Hard Working Man   I Was Sorry I Did Not Give Him The Last
Halfpenny I Had & Ask Him A Few Questions As To His Age & Name
& Parents   But Perhaps I May See Him Agen

Easter Monday – At The Easter Hunt I Saw A Stout Tall Young Woman
Dressed In A Darkish Flowerd Cotton Gown As A Milkmaid

142

PROSE
11–12 April, 21 April–30 May

Or Farm Servant & Stood Agen Her For Some Minutes Near A Small Clump Of Furze – I Did Not Speak To Her But I Now Wish I Had & Cannot Forget Her – Then I Saw Another Get Out Of A Gig With A Large Scotch Shawl On & A Pretty Face

[*between these two entries, the following is written and then crossed through*
Boxer Byron
made of Iron, alias
Box-iron
At Spring-field]

21 April–30 May

April 21ˢᵗ 1841
1 Weeks Labour – 2s/6d – Drawn 1s – 1s left 6d
April 27ᵗʰ   Recieved 1s
May 1ˢᵗ   Do   1s 6   2/6 left
May 3ʳᵈ   Do   6
Matthew Gammons over 5d a day –
Worked all the week & recieved only 6d – due or left 2s
May 10   Recieved 6d
May 14   Do for Song of Deborah 1s
                              Left 2s
May 18   Recieved 1s
May 22   Do   1
   Do for Child Harold – 1s 0
May 24   Recieved 1s
   Do 29   Do   1s
May 30   Recieved 1s
Monday   1s

PROSE
1 May, [May]

1 May

Jack Randalls Challange To All The World

Jack Randall The Champion Of The Prize Ring Begs Leave To Inform
The Sporting World That He Is Ready To Meet Any Customer In The
Ring Or On The Stage To Fight For The Sum Of £500 Or £1000 Aside
A Fair Stand Up Fight half Minute Time Win Or Loose   he Is Not
Particular As To Weight Colour Or Country   All He Wishes Is To
Meet With A Customer Who Has Pluck Enough To Come To The Sc[r]atch
                                                    Jack Randall
May 1st 1841

[beneath this advertisement, Clare adds, at a later date,
So let thine enemies perish O Lord]

[May]³

My Dearest Mary
    As This Will Be My Last Letter To You Or Any One Else – Let My
Stay In Prison Be As Long Or As Short As It May – I Will Write To
You & My Dear Patty In the Same Letter

[May – June]

My dear Wife Mary
   I might have said my first wife & first love & first every thing – but
I shall never forget my second wife & second love for I loved her once
as dearly as yourself – & almost do so now so I determined to keep you
both forever – & when I write to you I am writing to her at the same
time & in the same letter   God bless you both & forever & both your
familys also – I still keep writing though you do not write to me for if
a man had a wife & I have two –   but I tell it in a couplet with variations
as my poetry has been the worlds Horn book for many years – so here
it is

> "For if a husband will not let us know
> "That he's alive – he's dead – or *may* be so"
>
> [Truth must be truth & will where e'er we go
> Though bigots howl & fight to answer "No"
> *additional couplet added to draft version*]

No one knows how sick I am of this confinement possessing two wives
that ought to be my own & cannot see either one or the other   if I
was in prison for felony I could not be served worse then I am – wives
used to be alowed to see their husbands anywhere – religion forbids their
being parted   but I have not even religion on my side & more's the
pity   I have been rather poorly I might say ill for 8 or 9 days before
haymakeing & to get my self better I went a few evenings on Fern hill
& wrote a new Canto of 'Child Harold' & now I am better   I sat
under the Elm trees in old Mathews Homestead Leppits hill where I now
am – 2 or 3 evenings & wrote a new canto of Don Juan – merely to
pass the time away but nothing seems to shorten it in the least & I fear
I shall not be able to wear it away – nature to me seems dead & her very
pulse seems frozen to an iceicle in the summer sun –   what is the use

PROSE
[May – June], [mid-May? – July?]

of shutting me up from women in a petty paltry place as this merely
because I am a married man   & I dare say though I have two wives
if I got away I should soon have a third & I think I should serve you
both right in the bargain by doing so for I don't care a damn about
comeing home now – so you need not flatter yourselves with many
expec[ta]tions of seeing [me] nor do I expect you want to see me or you
would have contrived to have done it before now

[4]– My dear Mary take all the good wishes from me as your heart can
feel for your own husband & kiss all your dear family for their abscent
father & Pattys childern also & tell Patty that her husband is the same
man as he was when she married him 20 years ago in heart & good
intentions – God bless you both & your familys also   I wish you
both to keep in good health & be happy as I shall soon be when I have
the good luck to be with you all at home once again – the love I have
for you my dear Mary was never altered by time but always increased
by absence

I am my dear Mary
your affectionate husband
John Clare

[mid-May? – July?][5]

God almighty bless Mary Joyce Clare & her family now & forever – Amen
God almighty bless Martha Turner Clare & her family now & forever
– Amen

. . . .

Fern hill
At the back of the chapple a beautifull retreat from a mad house

. . . .

PROSE
[mid-May? – July?]

Scraps Fragments Quotations &c &c...

The word middling gennerally denotes something of a casuality – If the character of a woman is reckoned middling & she's a pretty woman the world genneraly look upon her as above the middlings but if she once gets below public opinion her character soon stinks & dies rotten

"Eternal Spirit God of truth to whom
"All things seem as they are."

. . . .

Speedily will be published

————————

The Sale of Old Wigs & sundries
A Poem by Lord Byron

————————

In Quarto 8vo & twelves

. . . .

In a short time will be Published

————————

A New Vol of Poems By Lord Byron
Not yet Collected in his works
Containing Songs New Cantos of Child Harrold
& ~~Scripture Paraphrases~~ additional Hebrew Mel[o]dies
~~Letters &c~~ Fragments &c

PROSE

[11–20 July?], 18–24 July

[11–20 July?][6]

My dear Eliza Phillips

Having been cooped up in this Hell of a Madhouse till I seem to be disowned by my friends & even forgot by my enemies for there is none to accept my challanges which I have from time to time given to the public I am almost mad in waiting for a better place & better company & all to no purpose   It is well known that I am a prize fighter by profession & a man that never feared any body in my life either in the ring or out of it – I do not much like to write love letters but this which I am now writing to you is a true one – you know that we have met before & the first oppertunity that offers we will meet again – I <have> am now writing a New Canto of Don Juan which I have taken the liberty to dedicate to you in remembrance of Days gone bye & when I have finished it I would send you the vol if I knew how in which is a new Canto of Child Harold also – I am my dear Elize

yours sincerely   John Clare

18–24 July

Reccolections &c of journey from Essex[7]

July 24th 1841   Returned home out of Essex & found no Mary – her & her family are as nothing to me now though she herself was once the dearest of all – & how can I forget

Journal Jul 18 – 1841 – Sunday – Felt very melancholly – went a walk on the forest in the afternoon – fell in with some gipseys one of whom offered to assist in my escape from the mad house by hiding me in his camp to which I almost agreed but told him I had no money to start with but if he would do so I would promise him fifty pounds & he agreed to do so before saturday   on friday I went again but he did not seem so willing so I said little about it – On sunday I went & they were all gone – <I found> an old wide awake hat & an old straw bonnet of the plumb pudding sort was left behind – & I put the hat in my pocket thinking it might be usefull for another oppertunity & as good luck would have it, it turned out to be so .

July 19 Monday – Did nothing

July 20 Reconnitered the rout the Gipsey pointed out & found it a legible one to make a movement & having only honest courage & myself in my army I Led the way & my troops soon followed but being careless in mapping down the rout as the Gipsey told me I missed the lane to Enfield town & was going down Enfield highway till I passed "The Labour in vain" Public house where a person I knew comeing out of the door told me the way
    I walked down the lane gently & was soon in Enfield Town & bye & bye on the great York Road where it was all plain sailing & steering ahead meeting no enemy & fearing none   I reached Stevenage where being Night I got over a gate crossed over the corner of a green paddock where seeing a pond or hollow in the corner I forced to stay off a respectable distance to keep from falling into it for my legs were nearly knocked up & began to stagger   I scaled some old rotten paleings into the yard & then had higher pailings to clamber over to get into the shed or hovel which I did with difficulty being rather weak   & to my good luck I found some trusses of clover piled up about 6 or more feet square which I gladly mounted & slept on   there was some trays in the hovel on which I could have reposed had I not found a better bed   I slept soundly but had a very uneasy dream   I thought my first wife lay on my left arm & somebody took her away from my side which made me wake up rather unhappy   I thought as I awoke somebody said "Mary" but nobody was near – I lay down with my head towards the north to

PROSE
18–24 July

show myself the steering point in the morning

July 21   [– when I awoke][8] Daylight was looking in on every side &
fearing my garrison might be taken by storm & myself be made prisoner
I left my lodging by the way I got in & thanked God for his kindness
in procureing it (for any thing in a famine is better then nothing & any
place that giveth the weary rest is a blessing)   I gained the north road
again & steered due north – on the left hand side the road under the
bank like a cave I saw a Man & boy coiled up asleep which I hailed &
they woke up to tell me the name of the next village[*]   Some where
on the London side the "Plough" Public house a Man passed me on
horseback in a Slop frock & said "here's another of the broken down
haymakers" & threw me a penny to get half a pint of beer which I picked
up & thanked him for   & when I got to the plough I called for a
half pint & drank it & got a rest & escaped a very heavy shower in the
bargain by having a shelter till it was over – afterwards I would have
begged a penny of two drovers who were very saucey so I begged no
more of any body meet who I would – I passed 3 or 4 good built houses
on a hill & a public house on the road side in the hollow below them
I seemed to pass the Milestones very quick in the morning but towards
night they seemed to be stretched further asunder   I got to a village
further on & forgot the name   the road on the left hand was quite
overshaded by some trees & quite dry so I sat down half an hour &
made a good many wishes for breakfast but wishes was no hearty meal
so I got up as hungry as I sat down – I forget here the names of the
villages I passed through but reccolect at late evening going through
Potton in Bedfordshire where I called in a house to light my pipe in
which was a civil old woman & a young country wench making lace on
a cushion as round as a globe & a young fellow all civil people – I asked
them a few questions as to the way & where the clergyman & overseer

---

[*] Baldeck [Clare's footnote; i.e. Baldock]

PROSE
18–24 July

lived but they scarcely heard me or gave me no answer[*]

I then went through Potton & happened with a kind talking country man who told me the Parson lived a good way from where I was or overseer I do'n't know which so I went on hopping with a crippled foot for the gravel had got into my old shoes one of which had now nearly lost the sole   Had I found the overseers house at hand or the Parsons I should have gave my name & begged for a shilling to carry me home but I was forced to brush on pennyless & be thankfull I had a leg to move on –

I then asked him wether he could tell me of a farm yard any where on the road where I could find a shed & some dry straw & he said yes & if you will go with me I will show you the place – its a public house on the left hand side the road at the sign of the "Ram"   but seeing a stone or flint heap I longed to rest as one of my feet was very painfull so I thanked him for his kindness & bid him go on – but the good natured fellow lingered awhile as if wishing to conduct me & then suddenly reccolecting that he had a hamper on his shoulder & a lock up bag in his hand cram full to meet the coach which he feared missing – he started hastily & was soon out of sight – I followed looking in vain for the country mans[9] straw bed – & not being able to meet it I lay down by a shed side under some Elm trees between the wall & the trees being a thick row planted some 5 or 6 feet from the buildings   I lay there & tried to sleep but the wind came in between them so cold that I lay till I quaked like the ague & quitted the lodging for a better at the Ram

---

[*] Note. On searching my pockets after the above was written I found part of a newspaper vide "Morning Chronicle" on which the followings fragments were pencilled soon after I got the information from labourers going to work or travellers journying along to better their condition as I was hopeing to do mine   in fact I believed I saw home in every ones countenance which seemed so cheerfull in my own – "There is no place like home"   the following was written by the Road side –
1st Day – Tuesday – Started from Enfield & slept at Stevenage on some clover trusses – cold lodging
Wednesday – Jacks Hill is passed already consisting of a beer shop & some houses on the hill appearing newly built – the last Mile stone 35 Miles from London   got through Baldeck & sat under a dry hedge & had a rest in lieu of breakfast [Clare's note. At the top of it, he writes 'This Note should be placed at the bottom of the page']

PROSE
18–24 July

which I could hardly hope to find – It now began to grow dark apace &
the odd houses on the road began to light up & show the inside tennants
lots very comfortable & my outside lot very uncomfortable & wretched
– still I hobbled forward as well as I could & at last came to the Ram
the shutters were not closed & the lighted windows looked very cheering
but I had no money & did not like to go in   there was a sort of shed
or gighouse at the end but I did not like to lie there as the people were
up – so I still travelled on   the road was very lonely & dark in places
being overshaded with trees   length I came to a place where the road
branched off into two turnpikes one to the right about & the other straight
forward & on going bye my eye glanced on a mile stone standing under
the hedge so I heedlessly turned back to read it to see where the other
road led too & on doing so I found it led to London   I then suddenly
forgot which was North or South & though I narrowly examined both
ways I could see no tree or bush or stone heap that I could reccolect I
had passed so I went on mile after mile almost convinced I was going
the same way I came   & these thoug[h]ts were so strong upon me that
doubt & hopelessness made me turn so feeble that I was scarcely able to
walk   yet I could not sit down or give up but shuffled along till I saw
a lamp shining as bright as the moon which on nearing I found was
suspended over a Tollgate   before I got through the man came out
with a candle & eyed me narrowly but having no fear I stopt to ask him
wether I was going northward & he said when you get through the gate
you are; so I thanked him kindly & went through on the other side &
gathered my old strength   as my doubts vanished I soon cheered up
& hummed the air of highland Mary as I went on   I at length fell in
with an odd house all alone near a wood but I could not see what the
sign was though the sign seemed to stand oddly enough in a sort of trough
or spout   there was a large porch over the door & being weary I crept
in & glad enough I was to find I could lye with my legs straight   the
inmates were all gone to roost for I could hear them turn over in bed so
I lay at full length on the stones in the porch – I slept here till daylight
& felt very much refreshed as I got up – I blest my two wives and both
their familys when I lay down & when I got up   & when I thought

152

PROSE
18–24 July

of some former difficultys on a like occasion I could not help blessing the Queen* – Having passed a Lodge on the left hand within a mile & a half or less of a town I think it might be St Ives but I forget the name# I sat down to rest on a flint heap where I might rest half an hour or more & while sitting here I saw a tall Gipsey come out of the Lodge gate & make down the road towards where I was sitting   when she got up to me on seeing she was a young woman with an honest looking countenance rather handsome I spoke to her & asked her a few questions which she answered readily & with evident good humour   so I got up & went on to the next town with her – she cautioned me on the way to put somthing in my hat to keep the crown up & said in a lower tone "you'll be noticed"   but not knowing what she hinted – I took no notice & made no reply   at length she pointed to a small tower church which she called Shefford Church & advised me to go on a footway which would take me direct to it & I should shorten my journey fifteen miles by doing so   I would gladly have taken the young womans advice feeling that it was honest & a nigh guess towards the truth   but fearing I might loose my way & not be able to find the north road again I thanked her & told her I should keep to the road when she bade me "good day" & went into a house or shop on the left hand side the road   I have but a slight reccolection of my journey between here & Stilton for I was knocked up & noticed little or nothing – one night I lay in a dyke bottom from the wind & went sleep half an hour when I suddenly awoke & found one side wet through from the sock in the dyke bottom so I got out & went on – I remember going down a very dark road hung over with trees on both sides very thick which seemed to extend a mile or two   I then entered a town & some of the chamber windows had candle lights

---

* The man whose daughter is the queen of England is now sitting on a stone heap on the high way to bugden without a farthing in his pocket & without [tast?]ing a bit of food ever since yesterday morning – when he was offerd a bit of Bread & cheese at Enfield – he has not had any since   but If I put a little fresh speed on hope too may speed to morrow – O Mary mary If you knew how anxious I am to see you & dear Patty with the childern I think you would come & meet me [Clare's note]
# It was St. Neots [Clare's note]

PROSE
18–24 July

shineing in them – I felt so weary here that I forced to sit down on the
ground to rest myself & while I sat here a[#] Coach that seemed to be
heavy laden came rattling up & stopt in the hollow below me & I cannot
reccolect its ever passing by me   I then got up & pushed onward
seeing little to notice for the road very often looked as stupid as myself
& I was very often half asleep as I went   on the third day I satisfied
my hunger by eating the grass by the road side which seemed to taste
something like bread   I was hungry & eat heartily till I was satisfied
& in fact the meal seemed to do me good   the next & last day I
reccolected that I had some tobacco & my box of lucifers being exausted
I could not light my pipe so I took to chewing Tobacco all day & eat
the quids when I had done & I was never hungry afterwards – I remember
passing through Buckden & going a length of road afterwards but I don't
reccolect the name of any place untill I came to stilton where I was
compleatly foot foundered & broken down   when I had got about half
way through the town a gravel causeway invited me to rest myself so I
lay down & nearly went sleep   a young woman (so I guessed by the
voice) came out of a house & said "poor creature" & another more elderly
said "O he shams"   but when I got up the latter said "o no he don't"
as I hobbled along very lame   I heard the voices but never looked
back to see where they came from – when I got near the Inn at the end
of the gravel walk I meet two young women & I asked one of them
wether the road branching to the right bye the end of the Inn did not
lead to Peterborough & she said "Yes" it did so   as soon as ever I
was on it I felt myself in homes way & went on rather more cheerfull
though I forced to rest oftener than usual   before I got to Peterborough
a man & woman passed me in a cart & on hailing me as they passed I
found they were neighbours from Helpstone where I used to live – I told
them I was knocked up which they could easily see & that I had neither
eat or drank any thing since I left Essex   when I told my story they
clubbed together & threw me fivepence out of the cart   I picked it up

---

[#] The Coach did pass me as I sat under some trees by a high wall &
the [lamps?] [flasshed?] in my face & wakened me up from a doze
when I knocked the gravel out of my shoes & started [Clare's note]

PROSE

18–24 July, 27 July

& called at a small public house near the bridge were I had two half pints
of ale & twopenn'oth of bread & cheese   when I had done I started
quite refreshed only my feet was more crippled then ever & I could scarcely
make a walk of it over the stones & being half ashamed to sit down in
the street I forced to keep on the move & got through Peterborough
better then I expected   when I got on the high road I rested on the
stone heaps as I passed till I was able to go on afresh & bye & bye I
passed Walton & soon reached Werrington & was making for the Beehive
as fast as I could when a cart met me with a man & a woman & a boy
in it   when nearing me the woman jumped out & caught fast hold of
my hands & wished me to get into the cart but I refused & thought her
either drunk or mad   but when I was told it was my second wife Patty
I got in & was soon at Northborough   but Mary was not there neither
could I get any information about her further then the old story of her
being dead six years ago which might be taken from a bran new old
Newspaper printed a dozen years ago   but I took no notice of the
blarney having seen her myself about a twelvemonth ago alive & well &
as young as ever – so here I am homeless at home & half gratified to
feel that I can be happy any where

> "May none those marks of my sad fate efface
> "For they appeal from tyranny to God"   Byron

27 July

To Mary Clare – Glinton

Northborough July 27 1841

My dear wife

I have written an account of my journey or rather escape from
Essex for your amusement & hope it may divert your leisure hours – I

PROSE
27 July, *after* 27 August

would have told you before now that I got here to Northborough last
friday night but not being able to see you or to hear where you was I
soon began to feel homeless at home & shall bye & bye feel nearly hopeless
but not so lonely as I did in Essex – for here I can see Glinton church
& feeling that Mary is safe if not happy & <I shall be the same> I am
gratified <to believe so>   though my home is no home to me my hopes
are not entirely hopeless while even the memory of Mary lives so near
me   God bless you My dear Mary   Give my love to your dear &
beautifull family & to your Mother – & believe me as I ever have been
& ever shall be

My dearest Mary
your affectionate Husband
John Clare

after 27 **August**[10]

[to Matthew Allen]

My dear Sir
    Having left the Forest in a hurry [I h]ad not time to take my leave of
you & your family but I intended to write & that before now   but
dullness & dissapointment prevented me for I found your words true on
my return here having neither friends or home left   but as it is called
the 'Poet's cottage' I claimed a lodging in it where I now am – one of
my fancys I found here with her family & all well – they meet me on
this side Werrington with a horse & cart & found me all but knocked up
for I had travelled from Essex to Northamptonshire without ever eating
or drinking all the way save one pennyworth of beer which was given me
by a farm servant near an odd house called the plough   one day I eat
grass to humour my hunger – but on the last day I chewed Tobacco &

never felt hungry afterwards – where my poetical fancy is I cannot say for the people in the neighbourhood tells me that the one called 'Mary' has been dead these 8 years[11]   but I can be miserably happy in any situation & any place & could have staid in yours on the forest if any of my friends had noticed me or come to see me – but the greatest annoyance in such places as yours are those servants styled keepers who often assumed as much authority over me as if I had been their prisoner & not likeing to quarrel I put up with it till I was weary of the place altogether   so I heard the voice of freedom & started & could have travelled to York with a penny loaf & a pint of beer for I should not have been fagged in body only one of my old shoes had nearly lost the sole before I started & let in the water & silt the first day & made me crippled & lame to the end of my journey

I had Eleven Books sent me from How & Parsons Booksellers <lent> some lent & some given me – out of the Eleven I only brought 5 vols here & as I don't want any part of Essex in Northamptonshire agen I wish you would have the kindness to send a servant to get them for me I should be very thankfull not that I care about the books altogether only it may be an excuse to see me & get me into company that I do not want to be acquainted with – one of your labourers Pratts Wife borrowed – 'Child Harold' – & Mrs Fishs Daughter has two or three or perhaps more all Lord Byrons Poems   & Mrs King late of the Owl Public house Leppits Hill & now of Endfield Highway has two or three all Lord Byrons & one is The 'Hours of Idleness'[12]

you told me somthing before haytime about the Queen alowing me a yearly sallary of £100 & that the first quarter had then commenced or else I dreamed so – [13] if I have the mistake is not of much consequence to anyone save myself & if true I wish you would get the Quarter for me if due* as I want to be independant & pay for board & lodging while I remain here – I look upon myself as a widow or bachellor I don't know which – I care nothing about the women now for they are faithless & decietfull & the first woman when there was no man but her husband found out means to cuckold him by the aid & assistance of the devil but women being more righteous now & men more plentiful they have

PROSE
after 27 August, [autumn?]

found out a more godly way to do it without the divils assistance & a man who possesses a women possesses losses without gain – the worst is the road to ruin & the best is nothing like a good Cow – man I never did like much & woman has long sickened me   I should [like] to be to myself a few years & lead the life of a hermit – but even there I should wish from one whom I am always thinking of & almost every Song I write has some sighs & wishes in Ink about Mary – If I have not made your head weary by reading thus far I have tired my own by writing it so I will bid you good bye

    & am My dear docter yours very sincerely   John Clare

* York & Co Peterborough or Eaton & Co Stamford [*Clare's note*]

give my best respects to Mrs Allen & Miss Allen & to Dr Stedman   also to Campbell & Hayward & Howard at Leopards Hill or in fact to any of the others who may think it worth while to enquire about me

[autumn?]

Recieved from C. Redding[14] while in Prison on Leopards Hill Eleven books two Given & the rest returnable – viz – Child Harold – Reddings Poems – & following lent viz Don Juan 1 Vol 5 Cantos – 2nd Part Cants. 6.7.8 Part 3rd Cants. 9, 10, 11 – Part 4th 12, 13, 14 – Part 5th Cants 15, 16

PROSE

[autumn?]

[autumn?]

[Self Identity][15]

A very good common place counsel is *Self Identity* to bid our own hearts not to forget our own selves & always to keep self in the first place lest all the world who always keeps us behind it should forget us all together – forget not thyself & the world will not forget thee – forget thyself & the world will willingly forget thee till thou art nothing but a living-dead man dwelling among shadows & falshood

>The mother may forget her child
>That dandled on her lap has been
>The bridegroom may forget the bride
>That he was wedded to yestreen

But I cannot forget that I'm a man & it would be dishonest & unmanly in me to do so

Self Identity is one of the first principles in everybodys life & fills up the outline of honest truth in the decision of character – a person who denies himself must either be a madman or a coward

I am often troubled at times to know that should the world have the impudence not to know me but willingly forgetting me wether any single individual would be honest enough to know me – such people would be usefull as the knocker to a door or the bell of a cryer to own the dead alive or the lost found   there are two impossibillitys which can never happen – I shall never be in three places at once nor ever change to a woman & that ought to be some comfort amid this moral or immoral "changing" in life – truth has a bad herald when she is obliged to take lies for her trumpeters – surely every man has the liberty to know himself

>Tis Liberty alone that gives the flower
>Of fleeting life its lustre & perfume
>& we are weeds without it.

PROSE

[October – November]

[October – November][16]

Autumn hath commenced her short pauses of showers calms & storms
& sunshine & shadow & with all her bustle she is nothing but a short
preface before a large volume of "Winter"   though not yet come to
drive us to the fireside He is giving us daily notice by dirty paths brimming
dykes & naked fields that he is already on the way – it is now very pleasant
to take walks in the morning & in fact at any time of the day though the
mornings are misty & "the foggy dew" lies long on the grass – here is a
drove leads us on its level sward right into the flaggy fens shaded on each
side with whitehorn hedges covered with awes of different shades of red
some may be almost called red-black others brick red & others nearly
scarlet like the coats of the fox hunters – now we have a flaggy ditch to
stride which is almost too wide for a stride to get over – a run & jump
just lands on the other side   & now a fine level bank smooth as a
bowling green curves & serpentines by a fine river whose wood of osiers
& reeds make a pleasant rustling sound though the wind scarcely moves
a single branch – how beautifull the bank curves on like an ornament in
a lawn by a piece of water   the map of ploughed field & grass ground
in small alotments on the left hand with an odd white cottage peeping
somewhere between the thorn hedges in the very perfection of quiet
retirement & comfort & on the right hand the clear river with its copies
of reeds & oziers & willow thickets   & now & then a house peeps
through where the willows are not so thick & showing trees loaded with
apples of a dull red & too thick for lodges shows we are near the approach
of a town   & now the church spire looking rather large dimensions
catches the eye like a jiant overtopping trees & houses & showing us his
magnitude from half way up the tower to the weathercock & looks noble
above his willow woods   nothing looks so noble among country
landscapes as church steeples & castle towers as fine houses & public
edifices do among city scenery – tis pleasant as I have done to day to
stand upon a length of Bridges & notice the objects around us   there
is the fine old Northborough castle peeping through the scanty foliage of

PROSE
[October – November]

orchards & thorn hedges & there is the beautifull Spire of Glinton Church towering high over the grey willows & dark wallnuts still lingering in the church yard like the remains of a wreck telling where their fellows foundered on the ocean of time – place of green Memorys & gloomy sorrows – even these meadow arches seem to me something of the beautifull having been so long a prisoner & shut up in confinement they appear something worthy of notice – to a man who has had his liberty they would appear nothing more then so many tunnels thrown over a few puddles that are dry three parts of the year but to me they are more interesting then a flight of arches thrown over a cascade in a park or even the crowded bridges in a great city – yonder is Maxey Tower church looking as if it was lighting up with sunshine when the Autumn sky is as gloomy as summer twilight & on the right peeping between the trees may be seen West Deepings crocketed spire & on the left Glinton Mill goes sweeing away to the wind – how sweet & green the banks wind along on each side the meadow with now & then a single arch crossing the meadow drain through which one can see a bit of the bank on the other side & being weary looking out for steeples I will take the path down the north bank its green slopes look so pleasant though the wind blows chilly & the rustics face looks purple with cold – men are occupied in cutting the weeds from the drains to make a water course for the autumn rains – solitary persons are sideing up the hedges & thrusting the brushwood in the thin places & creeps which the swine made from one ground or field into another & stopping gaps made in harvest by gleaners & labourers – the larks start up from the brown grass in the meadows where a couple of flutters & f[l]ights & drops out of sight as suddenly again into the grass – now a flock of redcaps seven or eight together take flight from the sides of the bank & settle again in the hedges which are almost crimson with awes seeming as if they fed on the seeds of the ragwort as no thistles are near – a solitary crow and sometimes a pair fly with heavy wing just over head now & then uttering a solitary croak to warn their tribes around that a man is approaching & then make a sudden wheel round at the sight of the stick in ones hand perhaps mistaking it for a gun – the top stones

PROSE
[October – November]

of the walls of the all the bridges I pass are full of two letter names rudely cut with a knife – spread hands – & feet – often true love knotts & sometimes figures meant for houses churches & flowers – & sheep hooks & some times names cut in full – the idle amusements of cowtending boys horse-tenders & shepherds – now a snipe with its pointed wings hurries up from the meadow dyke into the fields – the meadow lakes seen from the bank puts me in mind of school adventures & boyish rambles the very spots where I used to spend the whole sundays in fishing while the bells kept chiming in vain – I cannot make out where all these feelings & fancys are gone too – The plot of meadows now dont look bigger then a large homestead & the ponds that used to seem so large are now no bigger then puddles & as for fish I scarcely have interest enough to walk round them to see if there is any – yon arches yonder with trees peeping above them & between them & where the traveller is hopping away wearily over them on the narrow road is Lolham Brigs – time makes strange work with early fancys   the fancied riches & happiness of early life fades to shadows of less substances even then the shadows of dreams   I sigh for what is lost & cannot help it – yet there is even calm spots in the stormiest ocean & I can even now meet happiness in sorrow   the rural pictures or objects in these flats & meadows warms ones loneliness such as a rustic driving his little lot of cows or sheep down the plashy droves & plucking a handfull of awes from the half naked hedges to eat as he goes on – The rawky mornings now are often frosty – & the grass & wild herbs are often covered with rime as white as a shower of snow – in the fen greensward closes the pewet or lapwing may be seen in flocks of two or three hundred together about Waldram Hall dabbling on the hedges of the lakes left by the rains – it is pleasing to see the woods of osiers by the river side fading yellow   There are a few willow trees by the Hall or Cottage – where the crows sit in the old nests as if it was spring though perhaps they may do it to get from the cold for there is a little crizzling ice on the edges of the water in some places such as ruts & horsefeetings – Now the man is putting off his boat to ferry over the Water where an old passenger may now & then call to be ferried over

PROSE
[October – November]

the lake to the other bank or high road – the ozier hedges & holts are
with yellow & the white thorn hedges are getting thin of leaves & so
crowded with awes that bye & bye the fields will be dressed in nothing
but crimson & scarlet – nature like simplicity is beautifull in every dress
she chuses to put on with the seasons – even winter with his doublet of
snows & hoar frost can make himself agreeable when he chuses to give
people leave to go out of doors – I love to clamber over these bridge
walls & when I get off the banks on the road I instinctively look both
ways to see if any passengers are going or coming or carts or waggons
passing – now here is a stile partitioning off sombodys portion of the
bank but the middle rail is off so I stoop under to get through instead
of climbing over it – there is a pair of harrows painted red standing on
end against the thorn hedge & in another ground an old plough stands
on its beam ends against a dotterel tree   some times we see a roll lying
in on one corner & broken trays & an old gate off the hooks waiting to
be repaired till repairs are useless – even these rustic implements &
appendages of husbandry blend with nature & look pleasing in the fields

. . . .

Closes of greensward & meadow eaten down by cattle about harvest time
& pieces of naked water such as ponds lakes & pools without fish make
me melancholly to look over it & if ever so cheerfull I instantly feel low
spirited depressed & wretched – on the contrary pieces of greensward
where the hay has been cleared off smooth & green as a bowling green
with lakes of water well stocked with fish leaping up in the sunshine &
leaving rings widening & quavering on the water with the plunge of a
Pike in the weeds driving a host of roach into the clear water slanting
now & then towards the top their bellies of silver light in the sunshine
– these scenes though I am almost wretched quickly animate my feelings
& make me happy as if I was rambling in Paradise & perhaps more so
then if I was there where there would still be eves to trouble us

. . . .

PROSE
[October – November]

Gass Clouds

When a pipe is first lighted the smoke issuing from the bowl curls up in
distinct or seperate masses   this is the heated gass or gass smoke – &
we often see clouds which we identify by their curling up from the orison
in seperate masses as gass clouds which ascend into the middle sky &
then join the quiet journey other clouds & are lost in the same colour

. . . .

Insects in the chinese Rose Leaves (side stem leaves)

There is in autumn on the leaves of the chinese rosetree puncteres or
rather figures made in the form of serpents & though in different forms
or folds they all resemble each other in size & shape – one end being
the tale & the other the head of a silvery white – I could not make out
what sort of inscet did it as they had all punctered the skin of the leaf
& started

. . . .

The woods look pleasant in their autumn hues of brown & yellow – yet
the underwood stovens cut up last spring looks still green & vigorous as
summer – here is a furze bush in flower just at the woodgate & I can
see the green closes on the other side of the wood & the brown fallows
also between the thin saplings left standing

. . . .

How pleasant these wood rideings with the sward closely cut wind along
through the underwood that seems so entangled that you would wonder

PROSE
[October – November]

how the tall bracken contrives to get through it – brown & yellow leaves litter the greensward & rustles under the feet   the autumn tempest or winds sweeps through the vollying trees like the long mutterings of continued thunder or rollings of artillery a long way distant & yet the trees seem in no violent motion   but this low muttering thunder seems to be the sylvan voice of autumn   in walking through a wood even in what may be called a calm day for the season we may gennerally hear the same huzzing rumbling noise in the woods which to me is as agreeable as music – the stone pits on the heath with the stone piled up & the rubbish thrown in heaps covered in places with weeds & wild flowers growing rank & luxuriant looks very pleasing among the dark furze – here are heather bells of a bright blue bowing for shelter close by the cart ruts where the wind can scarcely come at them sheltered as if they had a house of their own   & in the woodrides are some dark purple flowers of Devils bit

. . . .

The starnels flock in the fields & make a loud chattering wether quarreling or playing I cannot tell but the harmony of nature is seldom interupted by bad feelings   the sparrows too flock & chitter in the neighbourhood of corn stacks which shepherd & other living almanacks say tokens bad weather

. . . .

The three Lolham bridges look very picturesque among the trees of which two are visible from the bank the first with four arches

. . . .

PROSE
19 October, 4 November, 17 November

19 October

Oct[r] 19. 1841 – William found a Cowslip in flower

4 November

4th Nov[r]   a immense flock of starnels settled on an ash tree in the orchard & when they took wing it was like a large roll of thunder

17 November

[to George Reid]

Novr 17 1841

Dear Sir

    When your Letter reached Northborough I was there also – having left Essex or rather made my escape from it on 23rd of July since which time I have never seen any company or made any visits anywhere Solitude being my chief society & nature my best companion   your enquirey to Patty after my health leaves me to say that I am very well that is as well as middling for my mind is as it always has been from a boy – a disappointment   I have never had the perusal of a Newspaper for some years & if you have any entertaining incidents in your Scotch Papers I should thank you for the loan of one now & then   could you give me any literary News   I myself left many Byron Poems behind me but I did not stay to know or hear what became of them & I have written some since I returned with an account of my escape from Essex – I was 3 Nights & 4 Days on the road without food & lodging but being used to rough voyages all my life it did not affect my health much only made me very lame in one foot from having a bad shoe on – the sole was

PROSE

17 November

nearly off when I started & its keeping on till I got here was little less
then a miracle – I am now more comfortable & remain Dear Sir
yours sincerely   John Clare

I think of Thee – A Song

I think of thee at early day
& wonder where my love can be
& when the evening shadows grey
O how I think of thee

Along the meadow banks I rove
& down the flaggy fen
& hope my first & early love
To meet thee once agen

I think of thee at dewy morn
& at the sunny noon
& walks with thee – now left forlorn
Beneath the silent moon

I think of thee I think of all
How blest we both have been –
The sun looks pale upon the wall
& autumn shuts the scene

I cant expect to meet the[e] now
The winters floods begin
The [win]d sighs through the naked bough
[Sad as] my heart within

I think of thee the seasons through
In spring when flowers I see

PROSE
17 November, 12 December

In winter's lorn & naked view
I think of only thee

While life breaths on this earthly ball
What e'er my lot shall be
Wether in freedom or in thrall
Mary I think of thee

12 December

Found a Cowslip in flower Decr. 12 1841

Notes

The major editions below are abbreviated in the notes, with other references given in full. The distinctive division of material in the book between *verso* and *recto* pages is followed in the notes.

JCOA   *John Clare*, ed. Eric Robinson and David Powell (Oxford Authors series, 1984).

JCBH   *John Clare By Himself*, ed. Eric Robinson and David Powell (Ashington and Manchester: Mid Northumberland Arts Group and Carcanet Press, 1996).

JCS   *John Clare: Selected Poetry*, ed. Geoffrey Summerfield
(Penguin)   (Harmondsworth: Penguin, 1990).

JCSP   *John Clare: Selected Poems*, ed. J.W. and Anne Tibble (London
(Everyman) and New York: Dent and Dutton, 1965).

JEJE   *John Clare: The Journals, Essays, and the Journey from Essex*, ed. Anne Tibble (Manchester: Carcanet Press, 1980).

Letters   *The Letters of John Clare*, ed. Mark Storey (Oxford: Clarendon Press, 1985).

LPJC (1964) *The Later Poems of John Clare*, ed. Eric Robinson and Geoffrey Summerfield (Manchester: Manchester University Press, 1964).

LPJC (1984) *The Later Poems of John Clare*, ed. Eric Robinson, David Powell, with Margaret Grainger, 2 vols. (Oxford: Oxford University Press, 1984).

NHPW   *The Natural History Prose Writings of John Clare*, ed. Margaret Grainger (Oxford: Clarendon Press, 1983).

PJCM   *Poems of John Clare's Madness*, ed. Geoffrey Grigson (London: Routledge & Kegan Paul, 1949).

1   *A Publisher and his Circle: the Life and Work of John Taylor, Keats's Publisher* (London: Routledge & Kegan Paul, 1972), pp. 86-128. This unfashionable view of Taylor's role has been recently supported in Zachary Leader, *Revision and Romantic Authorship* (Oxford: Clarendon Press, 1996), pp. 206-261, and in a review essay on Leader's book by Hugh Haughton in *John Clare Society Journal* (no. 17, July 1998), 65-73.

2   See *PJCM*; *JCSP* (Everyman); Salman Al-Wasiti, 'The Poetry of John Clare: a Critical Study', unpub. Ph.D. diss., University of Leicester, 1976; *LPJC* (1984), i.

3   *PJCM*, 16.

4   *LPJC* (1964), 25.

5   See, for example, the version presented in both editions entitled *Later Poems*. This version is also followed in *JCOA* and *JCSP* (Penguin).

6   A point implicitly made by Anne Tibble in *JEJE*, 24.

7   See my *'A Real World & Doubting Mind': a Critical Study of the Poetry of John Clare* (Pickering: Hull University Press, 1985), 218-23.

8   In fact, Clare's habit of capitalising goes back to 30 July 1840 at least, when a 'capitalised' song ('By A Cottage Near A Wood') was sent by Matthew Allen to a Rev. Thomas Wilkinson of Worcester (see *LPJC* [1984], i, 3-6).

9   The output of 1841 is to some extent anticipated by a set of 9 poems and fragments, and another of 20 completed poems, that were published in the *Overland Monthly*, x (February 1873), and the *English Journal*, 15 and 29 May 1841, respectively. No holograph manuscript of this material survives. *LPJC* (1984), i, 7-36, dates all the poems as '1840-1', with one definitely composed before 25 July 1840 ('The Forest Maid'). On balance, it seems probable that much of this material belongs to 1840 rather than 1841. No work from Clare's first two and a half years at High Beach (mid-1837 – beginning of 1840) now survives, even assuming any was written.

10 *'A Real World & Doubting Mind'*, 228-30.

11 Roughly 85% of the paraphrases are of material from the Old Testament. Significantly, the remainder are based upon the more apocalyptic parts of the New Testament (Matthew's vision of the Last Judgment, and the vision of the New Jerusalem in *Revelations*).

NOTES FOR VERSO PAGES

1   As indicated in the introduction above (p. x), roughly a third of the material for *Child Harold* exists in draft form only in MS 8, never being copied out into MS 6. Although the status of this draft as part of *Child Harold* is not incontrovertible, there are numerous continuities between the two manuscripts in terms of theme, tone, imagery and verse form; and most editors have adopted the material as part of the poem. Whatever the status of the MS 8 material, however, the songs and stanzas that appear there can be arranged in three basic ways, each of which is in several respects incompatible with the other two. The first is to arrange the verses according to the numbering that Clare provides, recognising from their cramped position between stanzas that such numbers were certainly added at a later date during 1841, and may not correspond with the actual sequence of composition. However, the numbering begins with a stanza 3 (there are no stanzas numbered 1 and 2), the figure 18 appears above two separate verses, and stanza 27 occurs at an earlier point in the manuscript than stanza 26. Three stanzas are not numbered at all. It is at least possible that these numbers were added hurriedly, perhaps shortly before his removal to Northampton.

    The second method is to present the stanzas simply as they follow each other in the manuscript, despite the clear evidence that Clare did not work methodically through the volume. It results in a sequence that then begins with the stanzas numbered 27, 3, 18, 4.

    The third pattern is to present first all the stanzas where initial letters are capitalised, and to follow them with those stanzas where normal upper and lower cases are used. There is considerable evidence (see p. xi above, and Al-Wasiti, 410) to suggest that Clare's practice of capitalisation is a distinct feature of *all* his writing between early spring and mid-May, after which period he reverted to normal usage. I follow Al-Wasiti in preferring this third method of arrangement, though we nonetheless differ in our positioning of a number of stanzas.

2   The semi-colon here is clearly unwanted.

3   Thus written by Clare, but clearly a slip for 'parted'.

4   The positioning of this stanza is problematic, since (as indicated in n. 1 above) there are two stanzas numbered 18 in MS 8. The Tibbles, Grigson, and Robinson and Powell, all place it after the stanza numbered 17 ('Nature thou truth of heaven'); and Grigson and the Tibbles, but not Robinson and Powell, then follow it with the *other*

stanza numbered 18. The problem with this arrangement, however, is that 'There Is A Tale' then appears as an isolated, capitalised stanza among verses where capitalisation has been discontinued. Furthermore, it abruptly and incongruously undercuts the affirmative mood of stanza 17 ('Spring came like God & turned it all to heaven'). In terms of both textual and imaginative logic, it seems more reasonable to place 'There Is A Tale' at this point. In sentiment, it is closely related to the despair of the preceding stanza ('For Loves However Dear Must Meet With Clouds'); and the following verse ('*Yet* Love Lives On') then provides a contrasting and more sanguine vision.

5   The positioning of this stanza is conjectural. Grigson and the Tibbles, but not Robinson and Powell, adhere to Clare's later numbering and place the verse immediately after the stanza numbered 26 ('Her looks was like'). However, this creates the same difficulty as noted with 'There Is A Tale' (see n. 4 above): 'The Paigles Bloom' then appears as an isolated, capitalised stanza among verses where upper cases have been discontinued. It is presumably for this reason that Al-Wasiti places the stanza as no.1 in his arrangement; and the references to 'The Paigles Bloom' and 'The Hedgerows Newly Leafing Thorn' clearly suggest a dating in spring. I place the stanza slightly later in the sequence because these two details might suggest a date of April or early May, rather than March; and because the notion of love's 'Blooms' in the preceding stanza is then taken up in the 'Paigles Bloom' of this verse. Clare quite often employs this kind of connecting strategy in the poem.

6   As can be seen, it is in the third stanza of this ballad that capitalisation is abruptly discontinued, corresponding to a similar change mid-poem in the biblical paraphrase *Song of Deborah*. There is nothing in the manuscript to prepare for, or explain, the change. It simply happens.

7   This stanza is interrupted in MS 8 by one of the earliest biblical paraphrases, *David's Lament*. The first five lines of the stanza appear on p. 62, and are completed on p. 64 after Clare's heading '24 Continued'.

8   The positioning of this stanza is conjectural. Robinson and Summerfield (*LPJC* [1964], 26-7) suggest that Clare may have intended the two stanzas following ('Hail Solitude' and 'Wrecked of all hopes') to function as an introductory apostrophe to the poem as a whole. Placing them as verses 1 and 2 would then allow 'Green bushes' to follow logically as stanza 3, particularly since the 'green trees' of the second verse would then be taken up by the 'green bushes & green trees' of stanza 3. Whether such an arrangement corresponds to the actual order of

composition, however, is more debatable. The absence of capitalisation suggests a dating after about mid-May, a conjecture supported by the references to the blossom of whitethorn and to 'the retireing solitudes of May'.

9 As already mentioned (see n. 1 above), there are two stanzas numbered 18 in MS 8.

10 All editors are agreed that this stanza marks a new section of the poem, since with the exception of the song 'Ive wandered many a weary mile', it is the first stanza to appear in the 'fair copy' (MS 6, p. 4), as well as the first verse in MS 8 (p. 3). Grigson, Robinson and Powell, and the Tibbles, all place it at the very beginning of their arrangements; but Al-Wasiti places it at the beginning of a new '[Summer Canto]' (for different interpretations of Clare's use of the word 'canto', see recto n. 16 below). From the repeated references to 'prison' and 'forest', and associated phrases, it is almost certain that this and the following eleven stanzas, ballad and song, were drafted during the early summer, before his escape from High Beach on 20 July, and after the capitalised stanzas already presented.

From this point onwards, I follow the 'fair copy' *text* of MS 6 (variant readings between draft and copy, which are generally minor, are cited in both versions of *LPJC*), but not necessarily the *sequence* of stanzas presented, since MS 6 does not always follow the probable chronology of drafting.

11 Despite the explicit dating of this poem by Clare, its position in the sequence is not incontrovertible. In the 'fair copy' of MS 6, it follows the stanza 'Cares gather round', as in the arrangement above. But in the drafts of MS 8, it appears *before* the stanza 'Mary thou ace of hearts'. If Al-Wasiti is correct in his surmise that 'This twilight seems' and the three following stanzas were written between 20 and 23 July (see n. 12 below), the placing of 'Written in a Thunder storm' *before* 'Mary thou ace of hearts' would imply that Clare wrote ten stanzas in a matter of five days, between 15 and 20 July. This is possible but not, on balance, probable.

12 Al-Wasiti places this and the following three stanzas in a group entitled '[On the Road to Northborough]', i.e. composed between 20 and 23 July. The pagination of MS 8 is of little help in verifying this conjectural dating, since 'This twilight seems' appears on p. 23 and the other stanzas on p. 6. In the 'fair copy' of MS 6, however, these verses do appear immediately after 'Written in a Thunder storm', dated 15 July. It is not unreasonable to suppose that the line 'Night finds me on

this lengthening road alone' has a strong literal, rather than simply a metaphoric, significance.

13 Clare's own note on this and the following song reads: 'a & b the above songs were written directly after my return home to Northborough last friday evening the rest of the stanzas & songs were written on Epping Forest Essex'. This dates the two songs to either 23 or 24 July.

14 The positioning of this stanza is conjectural. Grigson, Robinson and Summerfield, and the Tibbles, all place it immediately after the stanza 'This twilight seems', since it appears in that position in the 'fair copy' of MS 6. But it also appears in MS 7 on the same page as the song 'Heres where Mary loved to be', which can be firmly dated to 23 or 24 July (see n. 13 above). In sentiment, the stanza forcefully expresses Clare's turmoil at not finding Mary upon his return to Northborough – hence the tentative placing of it in this context.

15 cf. Coleridge, *The Pains of Sleep*: 'To be beloved is all I need, / And whom I love, I love indeed'.

16 In all previous arrangements, this and the following three stanzas have been placed rather later in the overall sequence, since they so appear in the 'fair copy' of MS 6. But there is considerable internal evidence to suggest that Clare may have drafted them soon after his return to Northborough, as an immediate response to seeing again the 'haunts of his youth' – schoolyard, walnut tree, thorn hedge, and so forth. The position of the stanzas in the draft of MS 7 is of no help in determining an earlier or later dating.

17 Al-Wasiti, following Grigson, places this as the first stanza in an '[Autumn Canto]'.

18 This stanza appears only in the 'fair copy' of MS 6, and was therefore certainly composed after 23 July.

19 This is the first stanza to draw upon the drafts of MS D20, and its positioning here is conjectural, the more so because it is clearly a paraphrase of *Isaiah* 57: 15. A draft prose version of this verse also appears in MS 8, p. 68, in what seems to be a different hand. It is possible that Clare copied out the verse into the *Child Harold* sequence mistakenly; but in the 'fair copy' of MS 6, it appears immediately after 'I love thee nature', without any visual or other break, even though there is no discernible connection between the two stanzas in idea, image or mood. Thematically, the verse bears some relationship to the vision evoked in the two preceding stanzas above, which has led to its tentative placing in this context.

20 In the draft of MS 7, this ballad occurs on the same page (p. 55) as the song 'Heres where Mary', which Clare certainly wrote on 23 or 24 July. But the last stanza of the ballad, with its reference to 'Now harvest browns the fen', suggests a dating rather later than July.

21 These are the first stanzas to draw upon the drafts of MS Don.a.8, and cannot therefore have been drafted before the beginning of September (see p. xii above).

22 This stanza occurs only in the 'fair copy' of MS 6, and was therefore certainly written after 23 July – a fact confirmed by the internal references to autumn and harvest.

23 This and the following stanza appear only in the 'fair copy' of MS 6, and were therefore certainly composed after 23 July.

24 This is the last stanza to draw upon the drafts of MS Don.a.8. In *LPJC* (1984), i, 68-9, Robinson and Powell follow this verse with a song ('Her cheeks are like roses') and an *unrhymed* stanza ('Honesty & good intentions') which appear in MS 6 among some miscellaneous prose passages, quotations and extensive biblical paraphrases that immediately follow 'The blackbird startles'. Grigson and the Tibbles include neither song nor stanza, whilst Al-Wasiti includes the song but not the stanza. The fact that Clare distinguishes these miscellanea by writing 'Child Harold' before the *next* stanza in the sequence, some 17 pages later, suggests that he did not intend either song or unrhymed stanza to be an integral part of the poem. (For a slightly different view, see *LPJC* [1984], i, 69).

25 This verse and the three stanzas following appear only in the 'fair copy' of MS 6.

26 These are the first stanzas to draw upon the drafts of MS A62.

27 This is the first stanza to draw upon the drafts of MS Don.c.64, which were almost certainly written after 11 November. Al-Wasiti places this stanza first in a 'Winter Canto'; and although there is no clear evidence that Clare intended it to introduce a fourth section of the poem, it seems almost certainly the product of these early winter months.

28 In terms of chronology of composition, this is almost certainly the last song Clare wrote for *Child Harold* before his removal to Northampton Asylum on 29 December. It is immediately followed in the 'fair copy' of MS 6 by the first thirty lines of his last biblical paraphrase.

NOTES FOR RECTO PAGES

1 The capitalisation of first letters in this fragment suggests a dating contemporaneous with the 'capitalised' stanzas of *Child Harold*, i.e. between March and mid-May.

2 The biblical paraphrases drafted during the spring (*Davids Lament &c, Israel Passing Over The Red Sea, Song of Deborah, [Psalm 104], Prayer of Habacuk, [Numbers 23]*, appear only in MS 8, and were not later copied into MS 6.

3 On p. 64 of MS 8, immediately after this two-line fragment, Clare notes '&c &c written April 30 1841'. By the side of the title, though distinctly separated from it, he adds 'written 1ˢᵗ of Hebrew Melodies'. It is probable that the '1ˢᵗ of [the] Hebrew Melodies' refers to *Davids Lament &c*, which would date it as drafted before the end of April.

4 A third of the way through this paraphrase, capitalisation is discontinued, corresponding to a similar change in the drafts for *Child Harold*. Almost certainly, the *Song of Deborah* was completed by 14 May, since Clare records having received a shilling for the poem on that day (see p. 142 above).

5 This paraphrase (*Numbers 24*) is a direct continuation of the one preceding (*Numbers 23: 21-30*), but unlike the earlier chapter, it is the first paraphrase to be copied into MS 6. There is no immediate reason why Clare should have chosen to copy the later but not the earlier part of the parable.

6 At this point in MS 6, Clare cites lines from Byron, himself, the Book of Job, and Dryden:

'Imputed madness prison'd solitude
& the minds canker in its savage mood' Byron

'If where thou art I may not dwell
'Twill sooth[e] to be where thou *hast been*' Byron

'Nature says 'Mary' but my pen denies
To write the truth & so it lives in sighs *[Clare]*

'They shall dig for death as for hid treasures & shall not find it' Job

'– O! would it were my lot
To be forgetfull as I am forgot – ' Byron

'I've now turned wild a commoner of nature
Of all forsaken & forsaking all' Dryden

The stanza 'Honesty and good intentions' then follows (see verso pages, n. 24, above), and the paraphrase resumes after the word 'Continued'.

7   These three miscellaneous pieces, the first of which is crossed through, appear only in MS 8, and were not later copied into MS 6. Their positioning here is conjectural, though the reference to 'summer', and the similarities between 'Nigh Leopards hill' and parts of *Don Juan*, clearly suggest a dating in early summer, before Clare's escape on 20 July.

8   In MS 6, p. 43, Clare indicates that four stanzas ('Milton sung Eden', 'The flower in bud', 'Marriage is nothing', and 'Love worse then debt') are to be inserted after this first verse of *Don Juan* (see n. 19 below).

9   If, as seems almost certain, this is an explicit reference to the defeat of the Whig party, it dates the stanza as June or early July. The motion of no confidence, in which the government was defeated, was moved by Sir Robert Peel on 5 June 1841. The election which confirmed the parliamentary defeat took place on 29 June.

10 As *LPJC* (1984), i, 92, notes, the marriage of Lord John Russell to Lady Fanny Elliott was announced as about to take place on 26 July in the *Northampton Mercury* of 12 June and 17 July.

11 As *LPJC* (1984), i, 93, points out, Albert's first absence from England was not in fact until March 1844. In *JCSP* (Penguin), 370, Summerfield takes this reference as possible evidence that Clare was revising the poem in that year. But rumours about Albert's unhappiness at court were rife during late 1840 and early 1841, and may well have included speculation that he was to return to Germany.

12 Melbourne did not in fact resign until 28 August, nearly two months after the Tory election victory, and nine days after parliament had reassembled with a Tory majority of 77. His leadership, though, had been in question for several months.

13 'The young princess' must refer to Victoria Adelaide, born 21 November 1840 (*not* 1841, as indicated in *JCSP* [Penguin], 370).

14 Ponders End, three miles to the west of High Beach and one mile from Enfield, would have been the first village passed by Clare after his escape on 20 July.

15 Eliza Phillips has never been identified, though her significance, real or imagined, is considerable. In the letter drafted to her immediately after *Don Juan* (MS 8, p. 13; see p. 147 above), Clare dedicates the poem to her 'in remembrance of Days gone bye'.

16 It is very possible that this stanza marks the beginning of the 'new Canto' that Clare speaks of in his letter to Eliza Phillips (see n. 15

above). The meaning Clare attaches to the word 'canto' has been variously interpreted, from Grigson's view that it represented, in *Child Harold*, a distinct imaginative section corresponding to the four seasons of the year, (*PJCM*, 16) to Robinson and Summerfield's opinion that the word means no more than 'a continuation of a poem' (*LPJC* [1964], 25). As ever, the truth may lie between these two extremes: that Clare conceived of a 'canto' as a clearly defined section of a longer poem (much as in his Byronic models), though without the specifying seasonal characteristics ascribed by Grigson.

17 Summerfield suggests (*JCSP* [Penguin], 371) that the two 'hells' may well refer to the colour of two of the three houses at High Beach asylum (Springfield, where the women lived, of red brick; Leopard's [or Leppit's] Hill, where the men lived, of stucco. The reference in the preceding line to the 'new road oer the forest' as 'the right one' might suggest that Clare had determined the route of his escape a number of days before it took place.

18 The 'next Tuesday', 13 July, is in fact Clare's birthday. The line presents one of the more striking examples of his identification with Byron.

19 These are the four stanzas that Clare indicates are to be inserted after the first verse of *Don Juan* (see n. 8 above). Three of the stanzas are first drafted in MS 7 and copied into MS 6, though one ('Love worse then debt') appears only in MS 6. It seems likely that all were composed just before, or soon after, the escape from High Beach.

20 Although the precise date of Clare's return to his biblical paraphrases is unclear, the first drafts in MS 7 (*Davids Prayer, Solomons Prayer &c &c*, and *Job 38: 1ˢᵗ Part*) may have been composed as early as August or September of the year. Drafts appearing in MS Don.a.8 (*The New Jerusalem, The River of the Water of Life, The Last Judgment, Lamentations of Jeremiah*, and *Job 39*) cannot have been written down before the beginning of September (see p. xii above).

21 These three miscellaneous fragments, which were drafted in MS A62 but not subsequently copied into MS 6, are tentatively ascribed to October or November.

22 This extensive series of paraphrases is drafted in MS Don.c.64, almost certainly no earlier than October. The first three paraphrases (*Job 40, Job 41, Psalm 19*) are followed immediately by the 'miscellaneous' poem 'Tis martinmass from rig to rig' (i.e. 11 November), which in turn is followed by the remaining paraphrases (*Psalm 91, Psalm 97, [Psalm 102: 1-17]* and *Isaiah Chap 47*). A number of them are then copied, in a more or less continuous sequence, into MS 6.

23 This rhyming version appears in Peterborough A62, at the beginning of the volume. The earliest date of composition is probably October.
24 Only the first thirty lines of this paraphrase were copied from MS Don.c.64 into MS 6. It seems very probable that Clare's copying was interrupted by his removal to Northampton (see verso n. 28 above)

NOTES FOR PROSE PAGES

1   As noted above (pp. 140-3), three different kinds of 'capitalised' prose (letter, note, and advertisement) are dated by Clare himself 17 March, Easter Sunday and Monday [11–12 April] and 1 May, supporting the view that capitalisation was a distinctive feature of all his writing between March and May.

2   Although there is no obvious connection between these two observations and the subject matter of *Child Harold*, the date indicates that the poem was clearly in Clare's thoughts at the time. Almost certainly, early stanzas had already been drafted. By 22 May (see p. 142 above), he had received a payment of a shilling 'for Child Harold'. This may have been for a completed section or 'Canto'.

3   The capitalisation in this unfinished draft letter points to a dating not later than about mid-May.

4   Storey (*Letters*, 647) suggests that this final section may have been written at a later date than the rest of the letter, presumably because of its changed tone of voice. In MS 8, however, the paragraph continues upon the one preceding without any indication of a break in composition.

5   These five fragments (prayer, natural observation, linguistic comment, and drafts for two advertisements) appear randomly in MS 8 on pp. 21, 25, 30, 32 and 39. They clearly reflect, however, major personal and imaginative concerns during the early weeks of the summer, and beyond.

6   In *Letters*, 647-8, Storey suggests a possible dating of May for this letter. In MS 8, p. 13, however, it follows immediately after the draft of *Don Juan*, the last six stanzas of which can be reasonably ascribed to the period 11 – 20 July. The fact that Clare amends a past tense to a present continuous ('I have written' to 'I am now writing a New Canto of Don Juan') might support a later, mid-July dating.

7   Clare's account of his journey out of Essex exists in a partially drafted, notebook form in MS 8, which was then used in copying out the full account into MS 6. Almost certainly, some of the material in MS 8 was actually written down during the journey itself. Understandably, given his circumstances, some of the dates provided are open to interpretation. The Sunday meeting with the gypsies, for instance, may have taken place on 4 or 11 July. The second Friday meeting may then have occurred on 8 or 15 July, with him returning to find them gone on 11 or 18 July. In the 'fair copy' of MS 6, the final entry of 24 July *prefaces* rather than concludes the account of the journey.

8 The phrase appears in the draft of MS 8, but is not copied into MS 6.
9 The draft of MS 8 ends at this point.
10 This letter is drafted in the margins and between the columns of the *Lincolnshire Chronicle and General Advertiser* for Friday 27 August.
11 Mary Joyce had in fact died only three years previously (on 16 July 1838), not eight.
12 Northampton MS 7, p. 55, contains a list, in the margins of the *Morning Chronicle* for 18 June, of 'Books Lent': 'Byrons Child Harold Mrs Pratt / Barn Houses near Sneston Essex / Don Juan – English Bards & Scotch Reviewers / Mrs Fish's Daughter at the Owl Leopards Hill / Hours of Idleness by Lord Byron – Mrs King Enfield / Highway – Middlesex'
13 The Queen Dowager had given 20 guineas towards a subscription fund set up in 1840; but the fund never reached its target of £500.
14 Cyrus Redding, editor of the *English Journal*, had visited Clare in High Beach in late April or early May. Two accounts of the meeting were published by Redding in the *Journal* for 15 May and 29 May (see *Clare: The Critical Heritage*, ed. Mark Storey [London: Routledge & Kegan Paul, 1973], 247-56).
15 This short prose piece about identity, which reflects many of the central concerns of *Child Harold*, appears on a page to itself in MS 6 (p. 23). It is certainly the product of the post-escape period, but there is nothing in the manuscript to establish the date of its composition more exactly.
16 These evocations of autumn scenes, which occur in MS 6 and MS A62, find many parallels of detail, phrase and tone in the later stanzas of *Child Harold* (see *NHPW*, 327, 329).

Further Reading

There is an increasing wealth of critical material relating to Clare, though with a significant emphasis in recent years upon the pre-asylum rather than the asylum work. In addition to the editions listed at the beginning of the notes, the following selected discussions provide helpful and often stimulating examinations of Clare's work during 1841. The list focusses upon explorations that are of article- or chapter-length at the very least, and upon work appearing within the last quarter of a century.

Al-Wasiti, Salman Dawood — 'The Poetry of John Clare: a Critical Study', unpub. Ph.D. diss., University of Leicester, 1976.

Barton, Anne — 'John Clare Reads Lord Byron', *Romanticism*, 2 (1996), 127-48.

Bates, Tom — 'John Clare and "Boximania"', *John Clare Society Journal*, 13 (July 1994), 5-17.

Brewer, William D — 'John Clare and Lord Byron', *John Clare Society Journal*, 11 (July 1992), 43-56.

Chilcott, Tim — *'A Real World & Doubting Mind': a Critical Study of the Poetry of John Clare*, Pickering: Hull University Press, 1985.

Cox, Peter — '"The Hearts Hid Anguish": Clare and Tennyson in Epping Forest', *John Clare Society Journal*, 13 (July 1994), 33-39.

Foulkes, Richard (ed.) — *John Clare: A Bicentenary Celebration*. Northampton: University of Leicester, Department of Adult Education, 1993.

Foss, Arthur, and Kerith Trick — *St Andrew's Hospital, Northampton: the First 150 Years (1838-1988)*. Cambridge: Granta Editions, 1989.

Howard, William — *John Clare*. Boston: Twayne Publishers, G.K. Hall & Co., 1981.

Martin, Philip W. — 'Authorial Identity and the Critical Act: John Clare and Lord Byron', in *Questioning Romanticism*, ed. John Beer. Baltimore: The Johns Hopkins University Press, 1995.

182

Minor, Mark   'Clare, Byron and the Bible: Additional Evidence from
                     the Asylum Manuscripts', *Bulletin of Research in the
                     Humanities*, 85 (1982), 104-26.
Pearce, Lynne   'John Clare and Mikhail Bakhtin: the Dialogic
                     Principle', unpub. Ph.D. diss., University of
                     Birmingham, 1987.
——   'John Clare's "Child Harold": a Polyphonic Reading',
                     Criticism, 31 (1989), 139-57.
Pedlar, Valerie   'John Clare's *Child Harold*, *John Clare Society Journal*, 8
                     (July 1989), 11-16.
——   '"No Place Like Home": Reconsidering Matthew
                     Allen and his "mild system" of treatment', *John Clare
                     Society Journal*, 13 (July 1994), 41-57.
Porter, Roy   '"All madness for writing": John Clare and the
                     asylum', in *John Clare in Context*, ed. Hugh Haughton,
                     Adam Phillips and Geoffrey Summerfield (Cambridge:
                     Cambridge University Press, 1993).
Schechter, Harriet   'The Limitations of Imitation: Byron, Clare and the
                     "Hebrew Melodies"', *John Clare Society Journal*, 4 (July
                     1985), 24-30.
Storey, Edward   *A Right to Song: the Life of John Clare*. London: Methuen,
                     1982.
Storey, Mark   'Byron and Clare: "Childe Harold" and "Child
                     Harold"', *Byron: Byronism – Liberalism –Philhellenism*,
                     Proceedings of the 14th International Symposium,
                     Athens (July 1987), 42-52.
Strickland, Edward   'Boxer Byron: A Clare Obsession', *The Byron Journal*,
                     17 (1989), 57-76.
Taylor, Catherine   '"The Resurrection of Child Harold": a Transcription
                     of Nor, MS6. and a Reconsideration of John Clare's
                     Child Harold and Related Writings', unpub. D.Phil.
                     diss., University of York, 1999.

Excellent guides to current and forthcoming work are to be found in the
John Clare Society Journal (1982 –), ed. John Goodridge, and on the Clare
web-site, ed. Simon Kövesi, at http://human.ntu.ac/clare

Index

Titles are indicated below in capitals, supplemented by untitled first lines in lower case.